AF371749

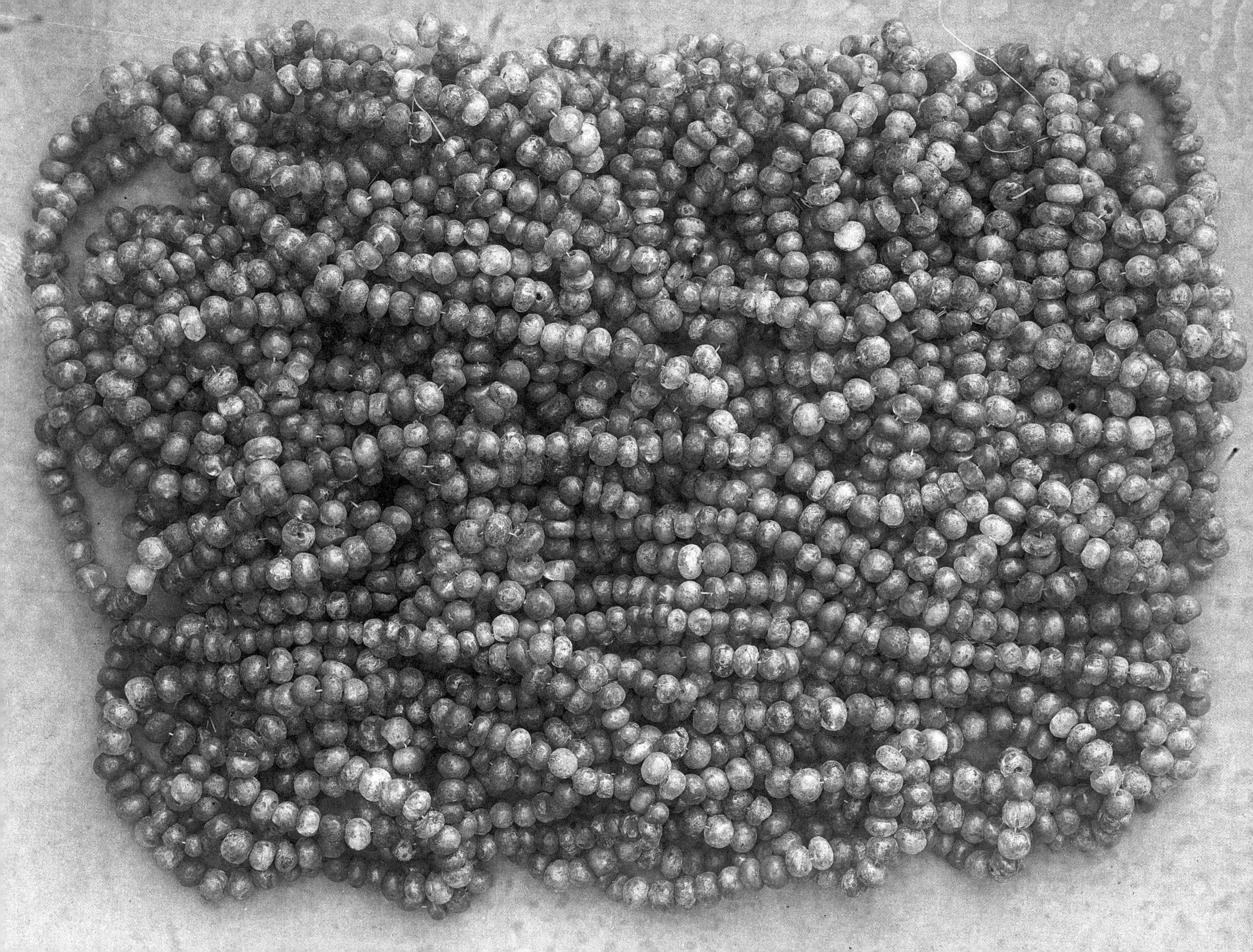

Unearthing Ancient Nubia

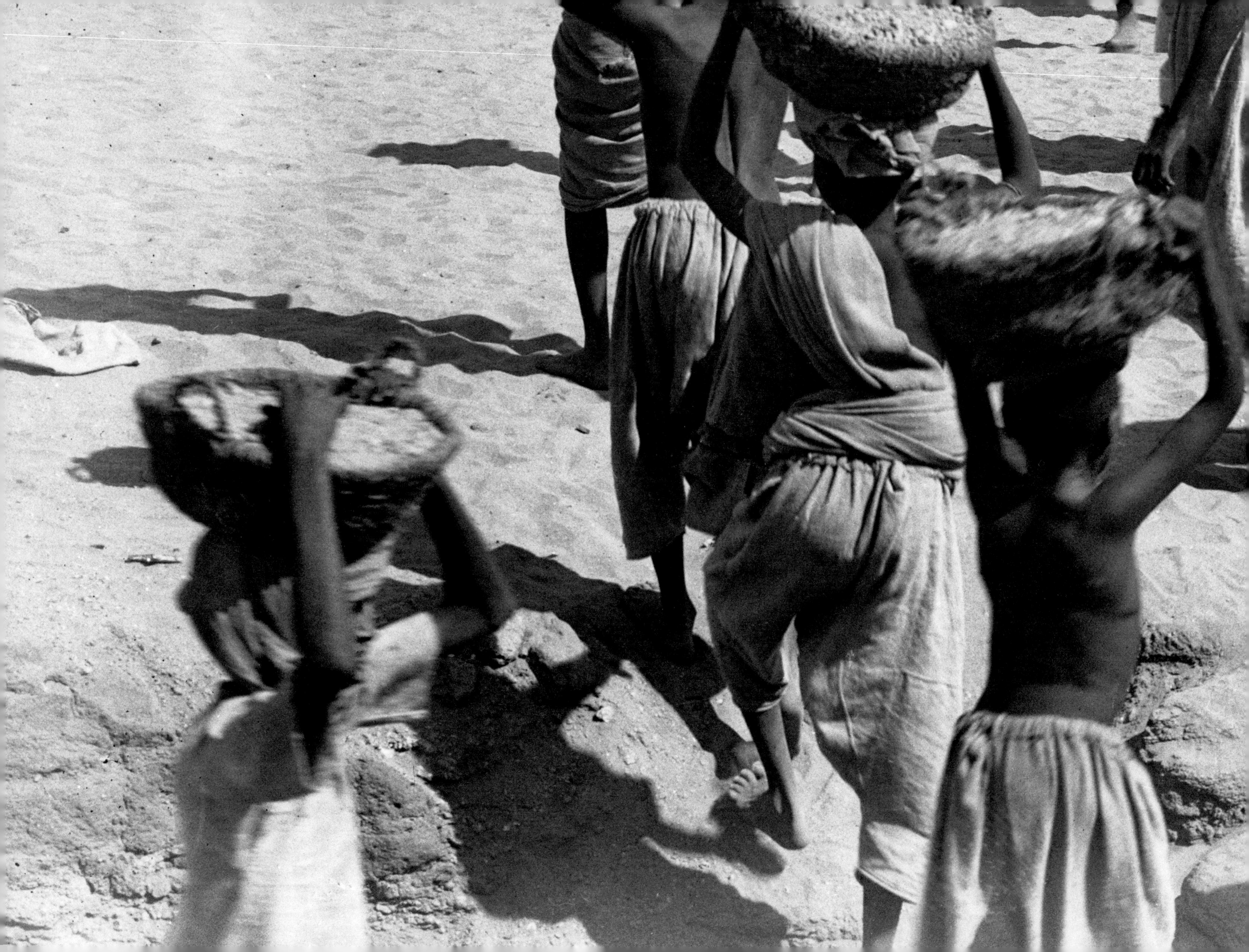

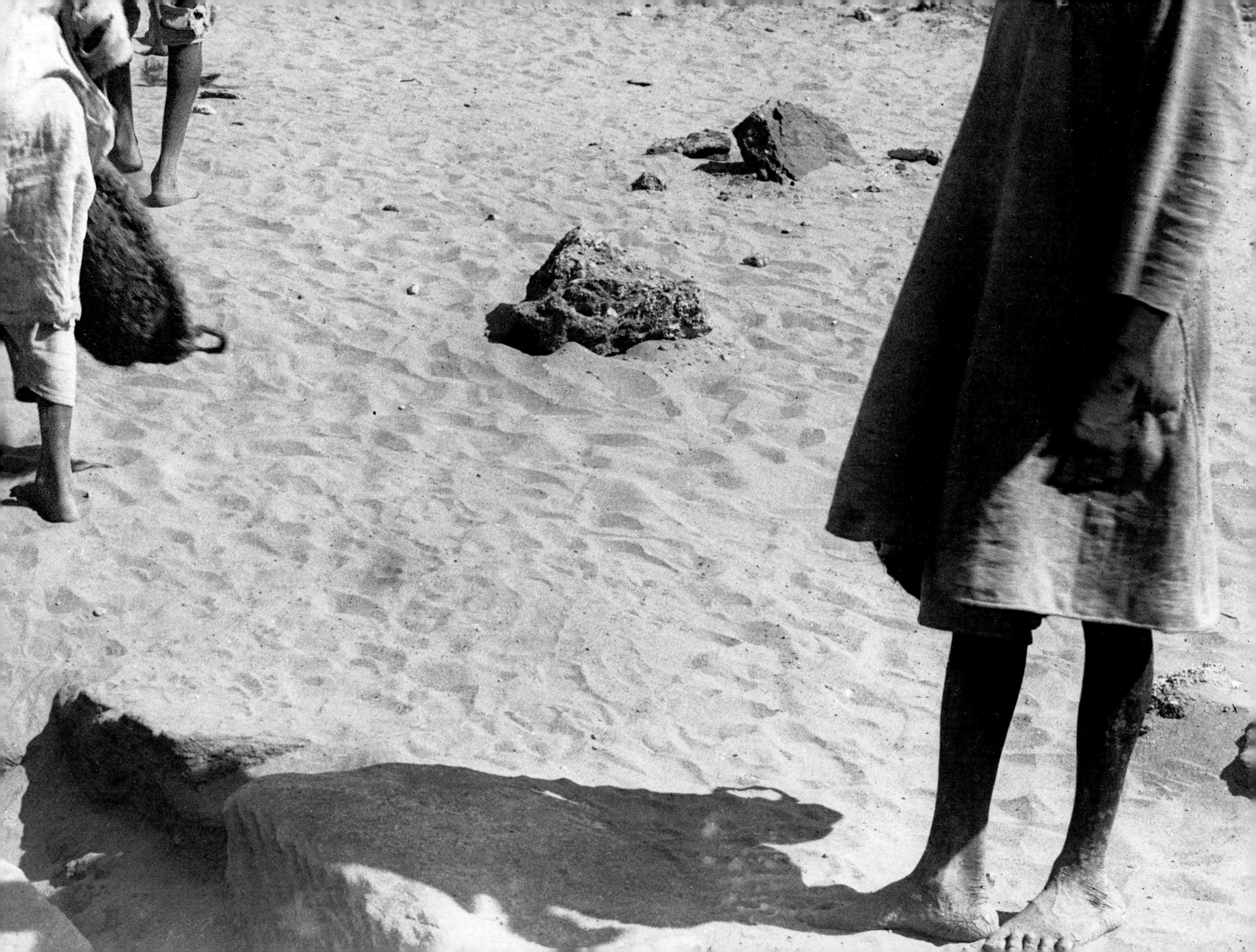

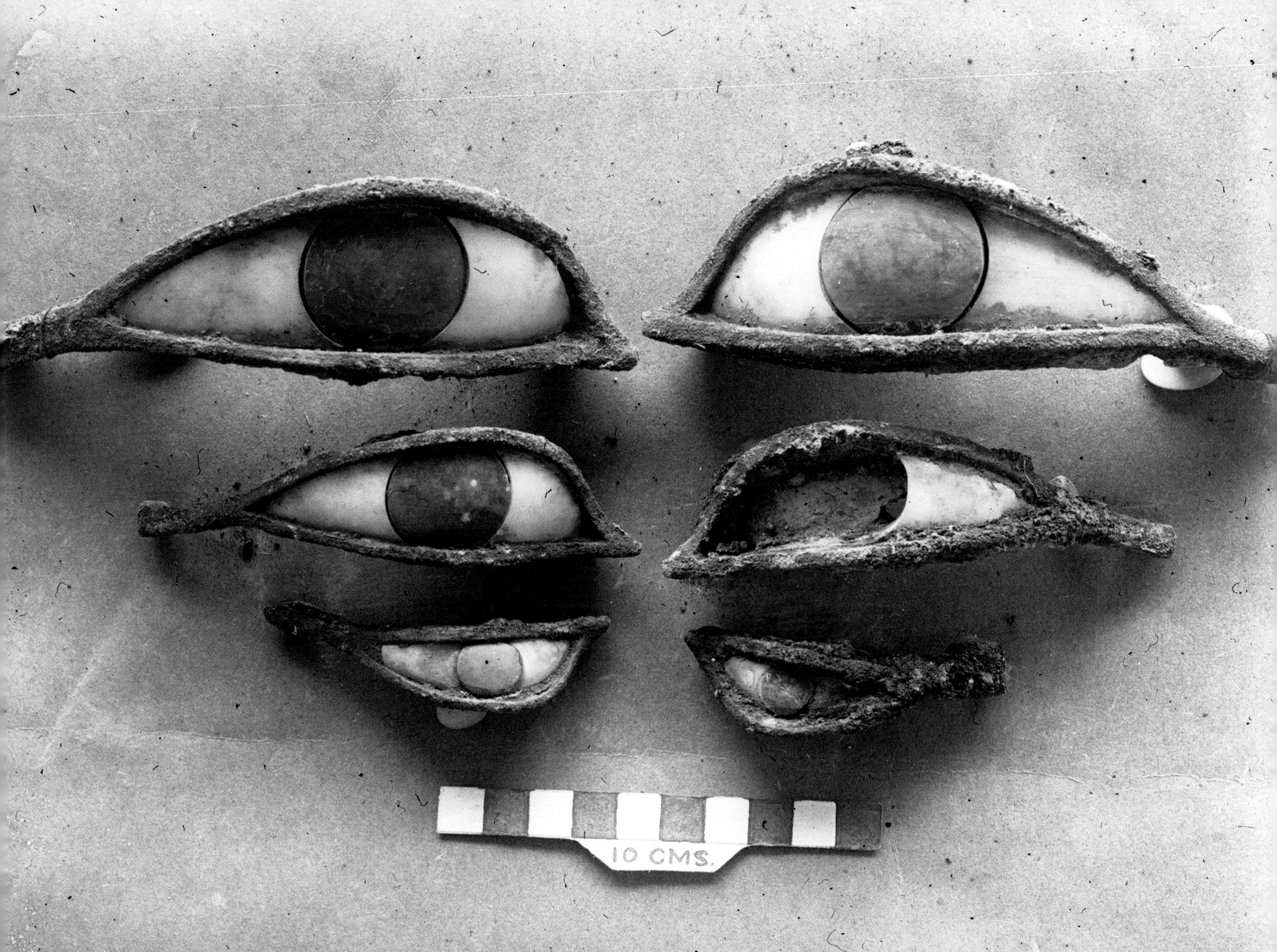
10 CMS.

It is April 27, 1916. We are at Gebel Barkal, Sudan. An over-life-size statue of an ancient ruler of the Nile stands on a dropcloth placed on the desert sand, ready to be photographed. The statue, recently unearthed from a pit beside the Great Temple of Amen, is made of stone and has been reassembled from fragments. The pieces fit together snugly but it is not clear what (other than their own weight) is holding them together. Behind the statue, five men hold up a backdrop made of several pieces of black cloth attached to two wooden beams. It is heavy. The men are clearly exerting themselves, their feet pressing against the light-rail tracks used for transporting carloads of excavation debris.

1

Workers stage photography of the granite gneiss statue of King Aspelta excavated at Gebel Barkal.
[Mohammedani Ibrahim Ibrahim]

The purpose of the photography session was to record the work of the Harvard University–Boston Museum of Fine Arts Expedition, which excavated ancient sites along the Nile over some forty years. George A. Reisner, the leader of the expedition, was keenly aware of the challenges of creating photographs under these conditions: "In judging the photographs," he wrote to the Museum's director, "remember that the statues had to be photographed in the glaring light of the tropics under great difficulties owing to the weight and size of the objects which made it nearly impossible to put the statues together." For publication, the statue would be isolated against its black background, removing all traces of how the image was made. Viewing these photographs in full, and considering them as images rather than documents, brings to life the landscape, the efforts of the workers, and the skill of the Egyptian photographers who recorded them.

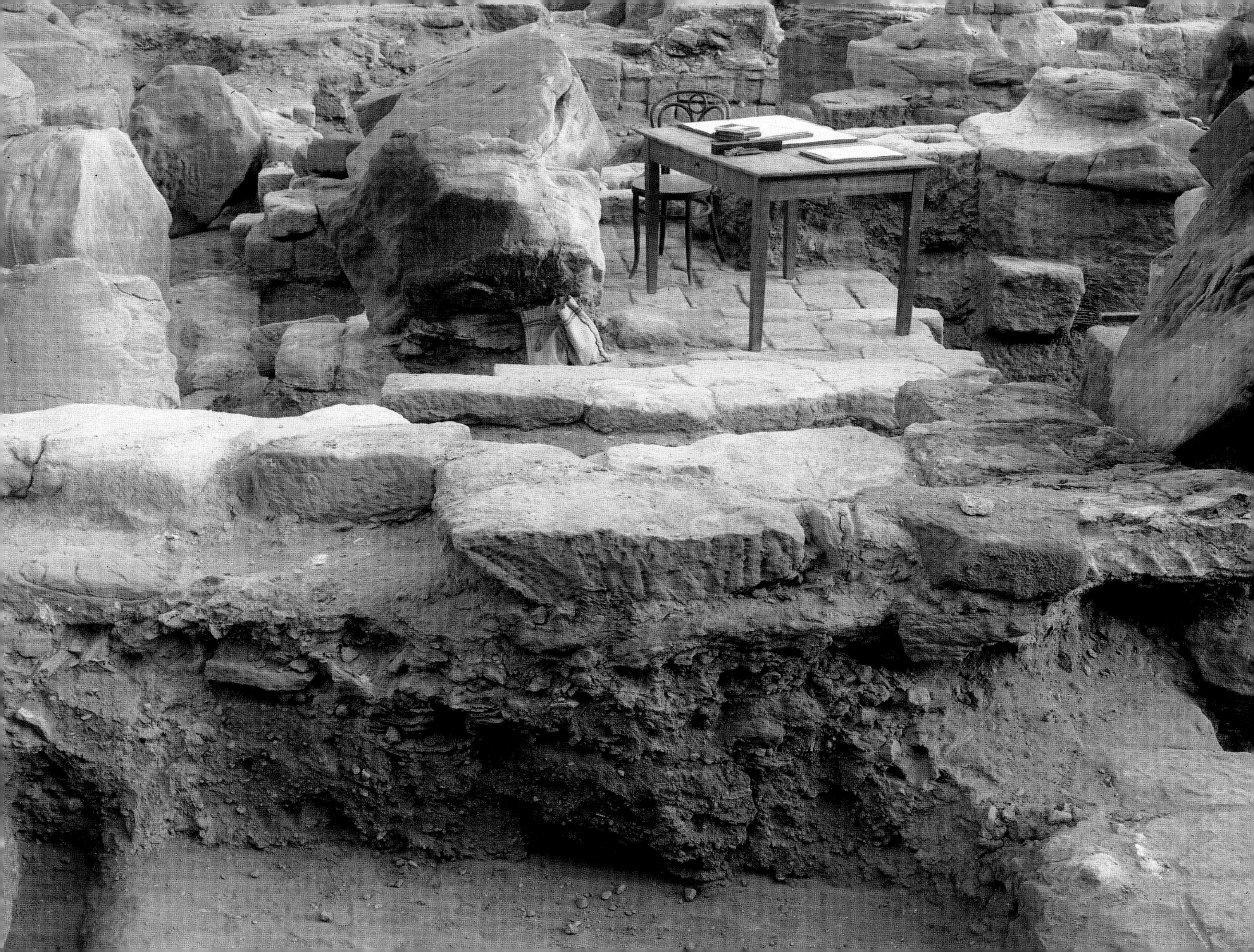

The Art and Science of Expedition Photography

13

On February 8, 1913, George Andrew Reisner, director of the Harvard University–Boston Museum of Fine Arts Expedition, arrived with twenty-nine trained Egyptian workers and their equipment at Merowe, the capital of Dongola Province in northern Sudan. Reisner planned to explore the ancient Nubian sites between Kerma, by the Third Cataract of the Nile, and the Egyptian border at Wadi Halfa, in order to select a site to excavate. Having obtained the necessary permissions, he and his team arrived at Kerma on February 11, and Reisner was so impressed by what he saw that they remained there until April. So began the Nubian campaign of the Harvard-MFA expedition, which continued almost without interruption until 1932. Over almost two decades it excavated the most important archaeological sites in northern Sudan—Kerma, Gebel Barkal, Nuri, Meroe (Begrawiya), and the Second Cataract Forts—and established the basis for all future work in the region. The images in this book are selected from roughly ten thousand photographs, preserved as glass-plate negatives, that record the expedition's pioneering work in northern Sudan.

The land of Nubia straddles modern-day Egypt and Sudan. Reisner's involvement with the area began in 1907, when he was asked by the Egyptian government to record and excavate all the ancient cemeteries along the ninety-five-mile stretch of the Nile Valley in Egypt—from Shellal south to Wadi el-Sebua—that were to be flooded when the Old Aswan Dam was heightened to increase the volume of water in the reservoir it contained. That project, known as the Archaeological Survey of Lower Nubia, focused on the early history of Nubia, as yet little known, and its relationship with Egypt, and resulted in the identification of a number of distinct cultural phases. The historical questions raised by the survey motivated Reisner to excavate in Sudan.

Reisner was a man of lofty principles and uncompromising high standards. For him, scientific work came first and objects came second: "It might appear from the inspection of the statues and reliefs sent to the Museum of Fine Arts that the search for works of art was the only object of the Egyptian Expedition; and yet, however important these things are from the Museum point of view, they can never be the sole object of an expedition which represents Harvard University as well as the Museum of Fine Arts. They are a partial product of fieldwork aiming also at historical research."[1]

1. George A. Reisner, "New Acquisitions of the Egyptian Department," *Museum of Fine Arts Bulletin* 12 (April 1914): 9.

Although Reisner was the head of a scientific expedition, he was also curator of Egyptian art at the MFA, and the Museum wanted works of art for the collection. Beginning in 1905, Reisner's work at the Giza pyramids had produced spectacular results, both in knowledge gained and in works of art for the Museum. Through the generosity of the Egyptian government, he had sent back to Boston masterpieces of Old Kingdom sculpture, the likes of which could be seen in no other museum outside Cairo. The MFA was not as strong in material from the Middle and New Kingdoms, because the Harvard-MFA expedition had never excavated an Egyptian site of either period. Northern Sudan—and specifically the area between Wadi Halfa and Merowe, which had been under Egyptian control during much of that time—was selected as a potentially rich source of Egyptian art.

Reisner reconciled the conflict between the demands of science and the desires of the Museum by maintaining that if the scientific work was conducted thoroughly and methodically, it would inevitably lead to the objects. The only element of chance lay in the selection of a site:

Then came one of those romantic experiences which sometimes fall to the lot of the excavator—a grinding period of seemingly hopeless drudgery, a painful reconstruction of the history of the place from broken bits and things, and suddenly, quite at the end, a revelation.…In a few days customs were shown to us such as were never known before in this period, a race was found whose possible identification one hardly dared confess to one's self, and objects were piled up in the storerooms such as I had never hoped to see. There were wooden beds with latticed thong covering and legs carved to imitate bull's legs (some of the legs cased in beaten gold), ostrich feather fans which could still be swung in the hand, swords with ivory and tortoise shell handles, scarabs of the Hyksos Period, a mass of brilliant black and red polished pottery as thin and fine as good porcelain.…

This trip shows very clearly how the expedition was guided partly by the need of fresh material, partly by printed information, and largely by chance, to select a site. The work at Kerma is an equally good illustration of how a site once selected is worked methodically through to completion in the face of apparently hopeless poverty of Museum results.[2]

2. Reisner, "New Acquisitions," 10.

15

An interviewer for the *Boston Post* in the spring of 1925, shortly after the discovery of the tomb of Queen Hetepheres at Giza, prompted Reisner: "I want to find out a little about you. In all the interviews so far published, there has never been anything about your personal experiences." Reisner replied that it was his own doing: "If you will study the reports of the expedition, you will discover that I have kept my own name out of them as much as possible. I am merely the director of a great enterprise, and the credit for whatever has been done belongs to the entire party."[3]

This party included not only the Americans and Europeans but also Egyptians. The Egyptian workers were highly trained and closely connected. They all came from the same area—the town of Qift and its vicinity, in southern or Upper Egypt—and many were related. The great British archaeologist William Matthew Flinders Petrie was the first to recognize the particular talent of the Quftis for excavation, beginning in 1893.[4] When Reisner started excavating in 1899 he had no field experience, so he sought the advice of experienced excavators who had worked with Petrie.[5] These men introduced him to the Qufti workers. Before long, Reisner could boast of having "the best trained and most effective gang in Egypt."[6] These were the men Reisner took with him to Nubia **(2)**.

Reisner was a pioneer in the use of photography to document every stage and every facet of archaeological fieldwork. In the beginning he took his own photographs and developed them himself. Assisting him in the darkroom was an Egyptian village boy, Said Ahmed Said, who quickly learned how to develop negatives and make prints. In 1901 Reisner turned over the darkroom work to him. By 1906 he had trained him to take photographs as well and made him responsible for all the photographic work of the expedition. In 1908 Said Ahmed was promoted to head *reis* (foreman); by that time he had started to train other boys, so from then on a succession of Egyptian photographers worked for the expedition. At a time when even Western-trained photographers were rarely credited for their work, Reisner proudly mentioned his Egyptian photographers by name in his publications.[7]

The photographers whose work is featured in this book are Bedawi Ahmed Abu Bukr, Mahmud Shadduf, Mohammedani Ibrahim Ibrahim, and Mustapha Abu el-Hamd. We know precious little about them. Bedawi Ahmed Abu Bukr attended the village school at Qift.

3. "Excavating Is No Soft Snap," *Boston Post*, Spring 1925.

4. Stephen Quirke, *Hidden Hands: Egyptian Workforces in Petrie Excavation Archives, 1880–1924* (London: Duckworth, 2010), 137–38, 234–35.

5. His advisers were J. E. Quibell and F. W. Green.

6. George A. Reisner, *The Early Dynastic Cemeteries of Naga-ed-Dêr*, part 1 (Leipzig: J. C. Hinrichs, 1908), vi.

7. George A. Reisner, *A History of the Giza Necropolis*, vol. 1 (Cambridge, Mass.: Harvard University Press, 1942), viii.

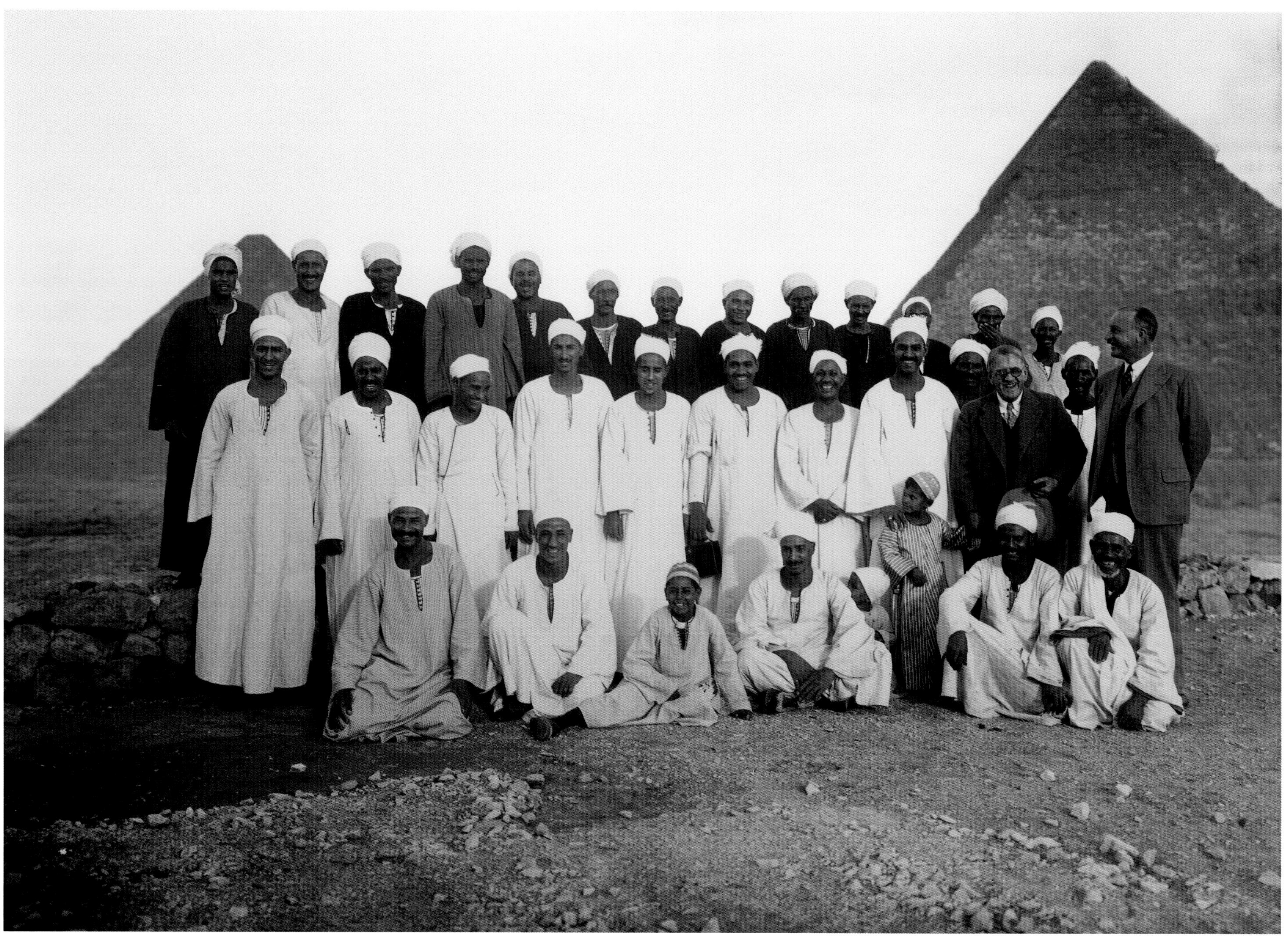

17

He joined the expedition as a boy in 1902 and was trained first as a photographer and later as a bookkeeper. He was promoted to photographer in 1906 and in that capacity accompanied Said Ahmed Said and Mahmud Shadduf to Lower Nubia in 1907.[8] From 1914 on, he also served as accountant for the expedition and kept all the books in Arabic.

Mohammedani Ibrahim Ibrahim attended the village school at Qift. He joined the expedition in 1906 and was promoted to photographer in 1914. Reisner called him "the most efficient of a long line of fellah boys trained by Said Ahmed who was the first (trained by myself)." The last of that line, Mohammedani was doing all the photographic work of the expedition by 1937 —taking pictures, making prints, and delivering prints and negatives to be registered.[9]

Mustapha Abu el-Hamd came from the village of Deir el-Ballas, across the Nile from Qift. Mustapha, his brother Ahmed, and two cousins joined the expedition between 1903 and 1906. A most versatile worker, Mustapha served in various capacities: photographer, excavator, houseboy, and finally, in his old age, guard at the Giza necropolis.[10]

The equipment involved was formidable: box cameras mounted on tripods, carriers for different size plates of film, multiple lenses, and tipping tables for angling the camera up or down (chiefly down, for graves or groups of objects). The photographers used a heavy, large-format camera capable of handling full-size glass plates (7 × 9 inches, about 18 × 23 cm) as well as half plates (5 × 7 inches, about 13 × 18 cm) and quarter plates (3 ½ × 4 ½ inches, about 9 × 11.5 cm). They also used a smaller camera for half and quarter-size plates only. The expedition had two of each kind of camera, one for use in the field, the other in camp.[11] The large format was preferred for general site views and landscapes. The wealth of detail and range of shading that could be captured by

8. George A. Reisner, *The Archaeological Survey of Nubia: Report for 1907–1908*, vol. 1: *Archaeological Report* (Cairo: National Printing Department, 1910), 10–11.

9. George A. Reisner, annotated curriculum vita, about 1937, MFA curatorial files.

10. George A. Reisner to Thomas Jefferson Coolidge, president of the Museum, December 23, 1933, MFA Archives.

11. Reisner's manuscript of instructions was edited by Peter Der Manuelian and published as "George Andrew Reisner on Archaeological Photography," *Journal of the American Research Center in Egypt* 29 (1992): 1–34.

2

Staff at Harvard Camp, the expedition's headquarters by the Giza pyramids in Egypt. The MFA president George H. Edgell and George Reisner are in the middle row (right and second from right). The photographer Mustapha Abu el-Hamd is seated in the front row, fourth from left. [Mohammedani Ibrahim Ibrahim]

an experienced photographer is astonishing. For informal shots of the men at work, of people and places encountered on their travels, of incidents at camp, and of themselves, the photographers used a small-format hand-held Kodak camera. For our purposes these images are often among the most interesting.

When necessary, the photographers could convert a rock-cut tomb or stone quarry into a darkroom, but purpose-built darkrooms were set up wherever the expedition was working on a regular basis, either at Harvard Camp, the expedition's headquarters by the Giza pyramids, or in Sudan. Images of the excavations themselves obviously could be taken only at the site; smaller finds could be photographed anywhere, and objects from Sudan were often photographed at Giza. A snapshot taken by Reisner in 1916 shows the photographer Mahmud Shadduf in front of Harvard Camp, contact-printing glass-plate negatives on printing-out paper through direct exposure to sunlight, assisted by a puppy named Patrick Cheops **(3)**.

These photographs were not taken for commercial purposes or as art. They were taken specifically to record the progress and the results of the excavations, and their highest destiny was to be reproduced in the published excavation report. Reisner gave detailed instructions on how to photograph an archaeological site. After the plates were developed and approved, two sets of prints were made. One set was filed numerically by size, and the other set was mounted on cardboard and organized by site, comprising views of the excavations and the objects photographed in camp, to be annotated by the archaeologists. Selected images were then chosen to be reproduced in scholarly journals and eventually, after being cropped to show only what was needed to illustrate the point, in the final excavation reports.

3
Mohammed Shadduf contact-printing photographs through direct exposure to sunlight, with puppy "Patrick Cheops," at Harvard Camp. [George Andrew Reisner]

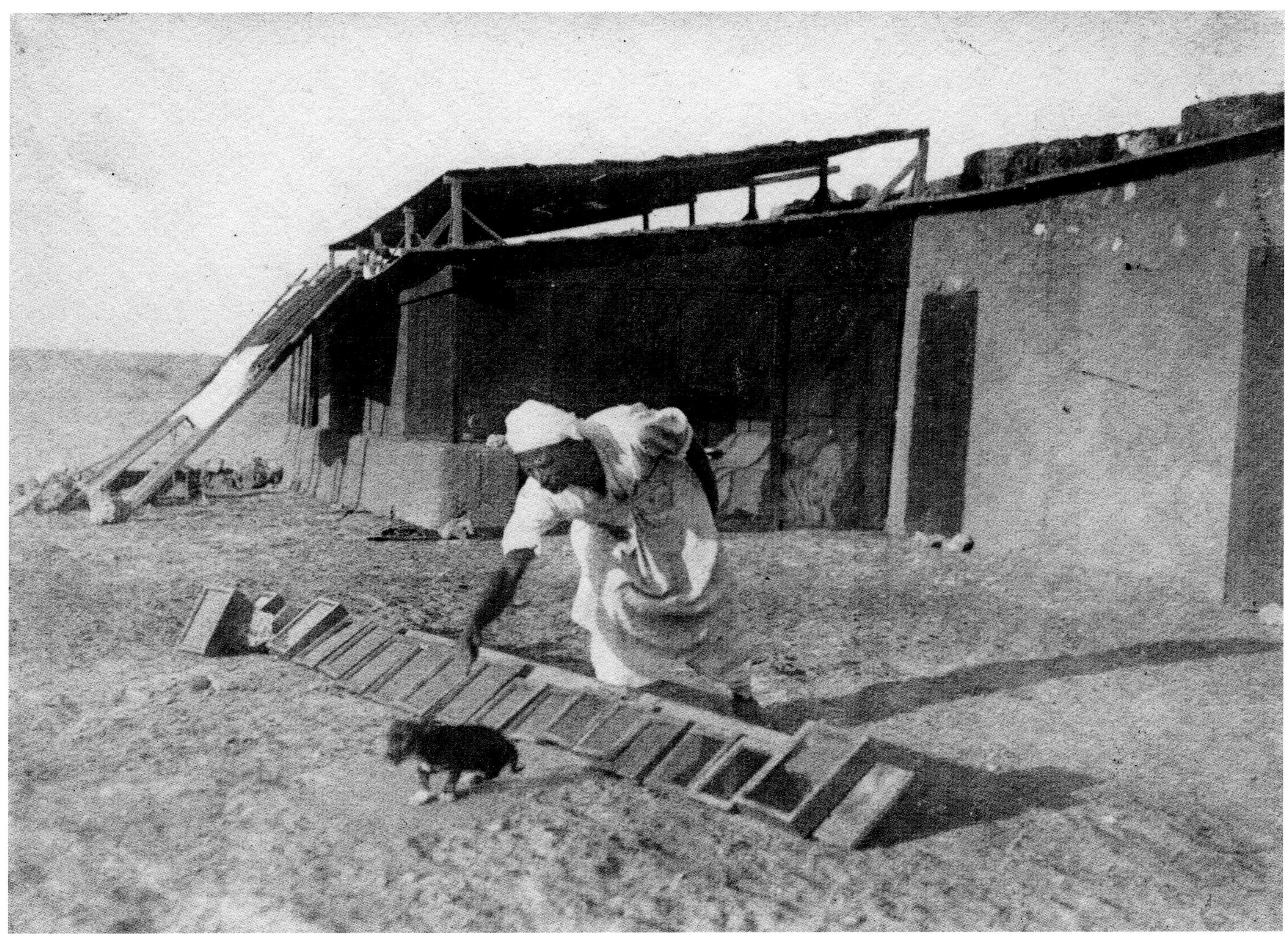

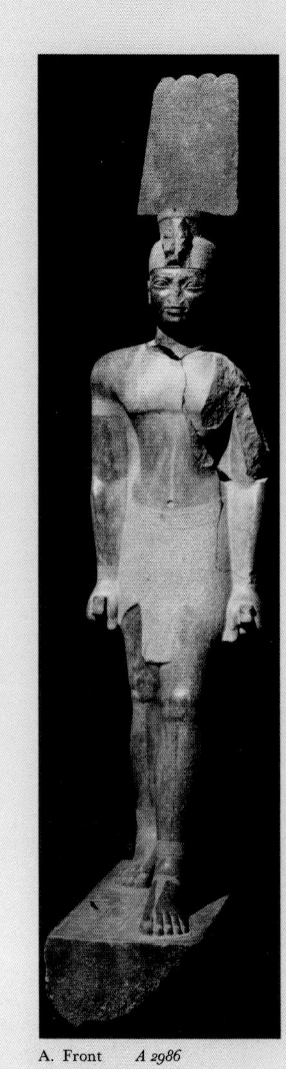

A. Front   *A 2986*

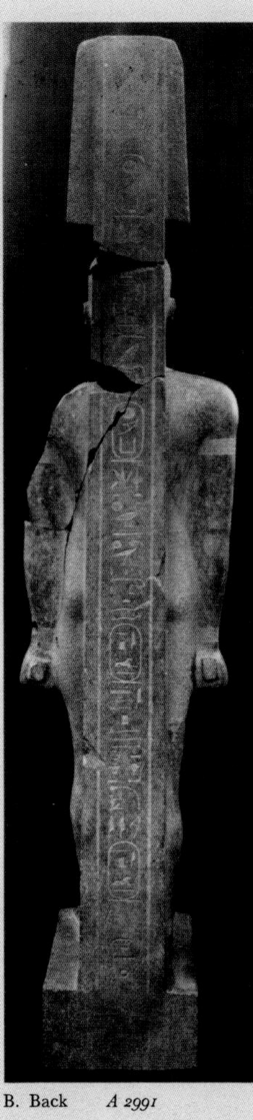

B. Back   *A 2991*

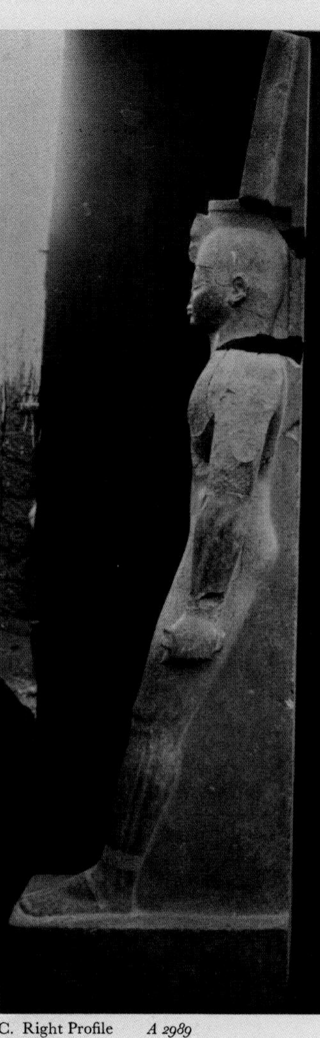

C. Right Profile   *A 2989*

Granite Statue of Aspelta. MFA 23.730

PLATE XXI

Reisner could be confident that his photographers were following his instructions as a matter of habit. But the photographers, having mastered their craft and developed a feel for composition, inevitably brought their artistic sensibility into play when recording a landscape or arranging objects in a pleasing design. Their inventive and eye-catching arrays of small finds, such as amulets, scarabs, and jewelry, recall earlier methods of aesthetic rather than archaeological museum installations—such as those done by Auguste Mariette for the Bulaq Museum, the forerunner of today's Egyptian Museum, Cairo—yet they fulfill every requirement of science.[12]

When these images are viewed in their entirety, uncropped, they reveal a wealth of information about how they were made. In the excavation report, a photograph of the colossal statue of King Aspelta is closely cropped so that the figure appears against a solid black background—both so as not to distract from the subject and to illustrate three views of the object side by side on one page (**4**; see also **67**).[13] The statue exists alone, in the abstract. Gone are the storage jars leaning against the mudbrick walls of the house, the packing crates, the barely perceptible edge of the man standing behind the backcloth, and the palm trees in the background, which give such a vivid sense of place and also of scale. Likewise, the scenic view across the Semna cataract (**5**) in its published format was cropped horizontally to show only the relationship between the two forts and to fit three views one above another on a single page.[14] Uncropped, the view is so much more expansive, with the desert in the foreground and the sky above—in fact, it is a beautiful photograph.

Showing the best of these images complete, outside their original strictly documentary context, brings the settings in which they were made to life and reveals the artistry of their makers. In these photographs, scientific rigor and artistic perception happily coexist.

12. Donald Malcolm Reid, *Whose Pharaohs? Archaeology, Museums, and Egyptian National Identity from Napoleon to World War I* (Berkeley: University of California Press, 2002), 106–7.

13. Dows Dunham, *The Barkal Temples* (Boston: Museum of Fine Arts, 1970), pl. XXI.

14. Dows Dunham and Jozef M. A. Janssen, *Second Cataract Forts*, vol. 1: *Semna Kumma* (Boston: Museum of Fine Arts, 1960), pl. 1.

4
Plate from the published expedition report showing multiple views of the statue of Aspelta.

5

At the southern end of the Second Cataract, the Nile passes through a narrow gorge. Perched high upon the rocks on either side, a pair of mighty fortresses—Semna on the west (at right) and Kumma on the east—guarded Egypt's southern boundary. So rugged and inhospitable is the landscape that the area is called the Batn el-Hagar, or "Belly of Rocks." [Mohammedani Ibrahim Ibrahim]

6 [overleaf]

About three miles (five kilometers) north of Semna is the island of Uronarti. At its highest point is another fortress, with mighty ramparts built of mudbrick strengthened by wooden beams. Highly visible symbols of Egypt's might, the Second Cataract Forts were part of a highly organized and interconnected system of defense that protected the border and regulated trade both by river and by land. [Mustapha Abu el-Hamd]

7 [overleaf]

Erected in the nineteenth century BC during Egypt's Twelfth Dynasty, the forts were reoccupied in the sixteenth century BC, when all of Nubia as far as the Fifth Cataract of the Nile was brought under Egyptian control. Inside the fortress of Semna, Thutmose III (r. 1479–1425 BC) built this small temple dedicated to the god Dedun and the deified Twelfth Dynasty king Senwosret III, who established Semna as Egypt's southern border three hundred years earlier. Favored by travelers and photographers, the temple was dismantled in the 1960s and moved to Khartoum so it would not be flooded by the Aswan High Dam. [Mohammedani Ibrahim Ibrahim]

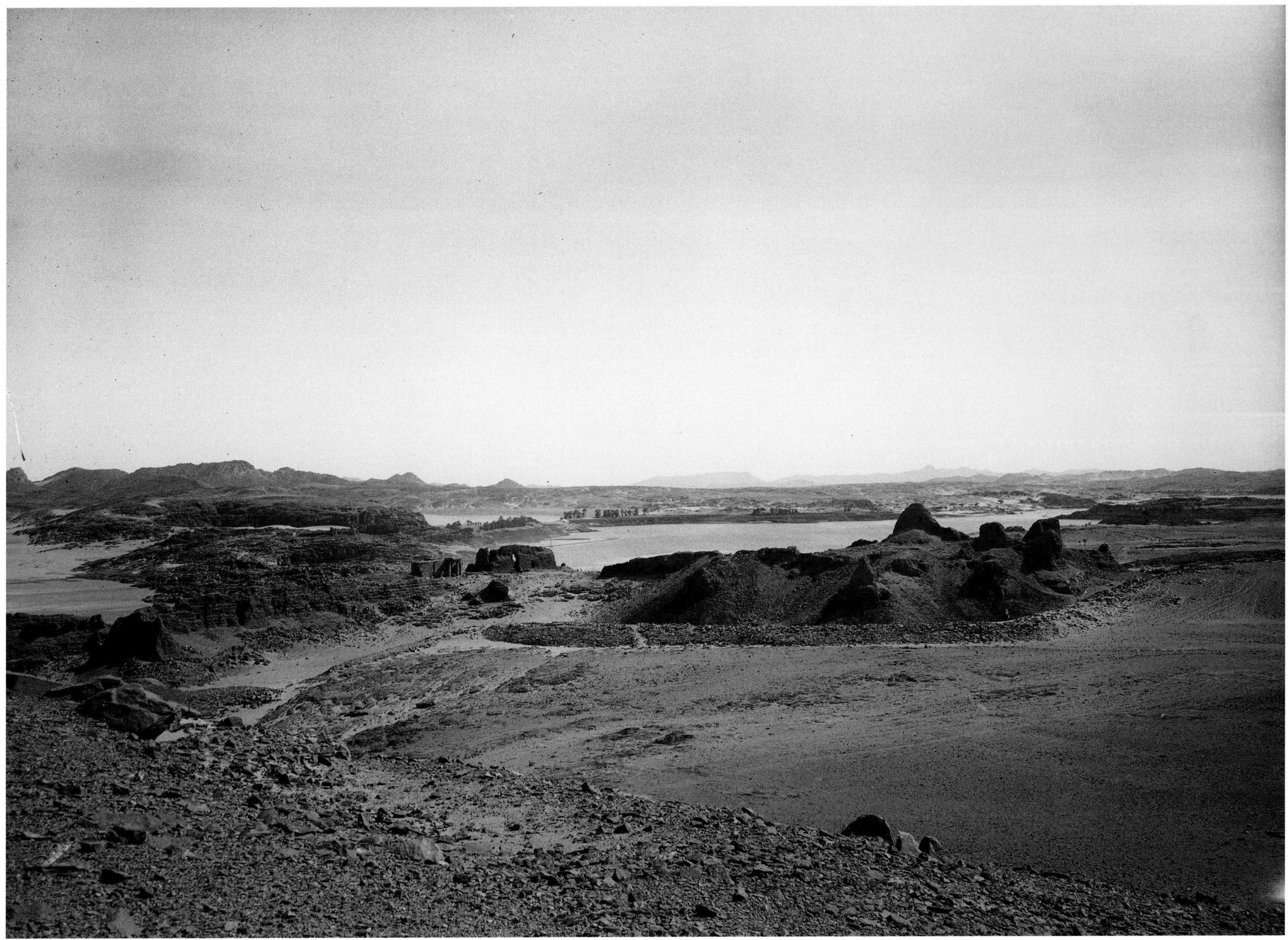

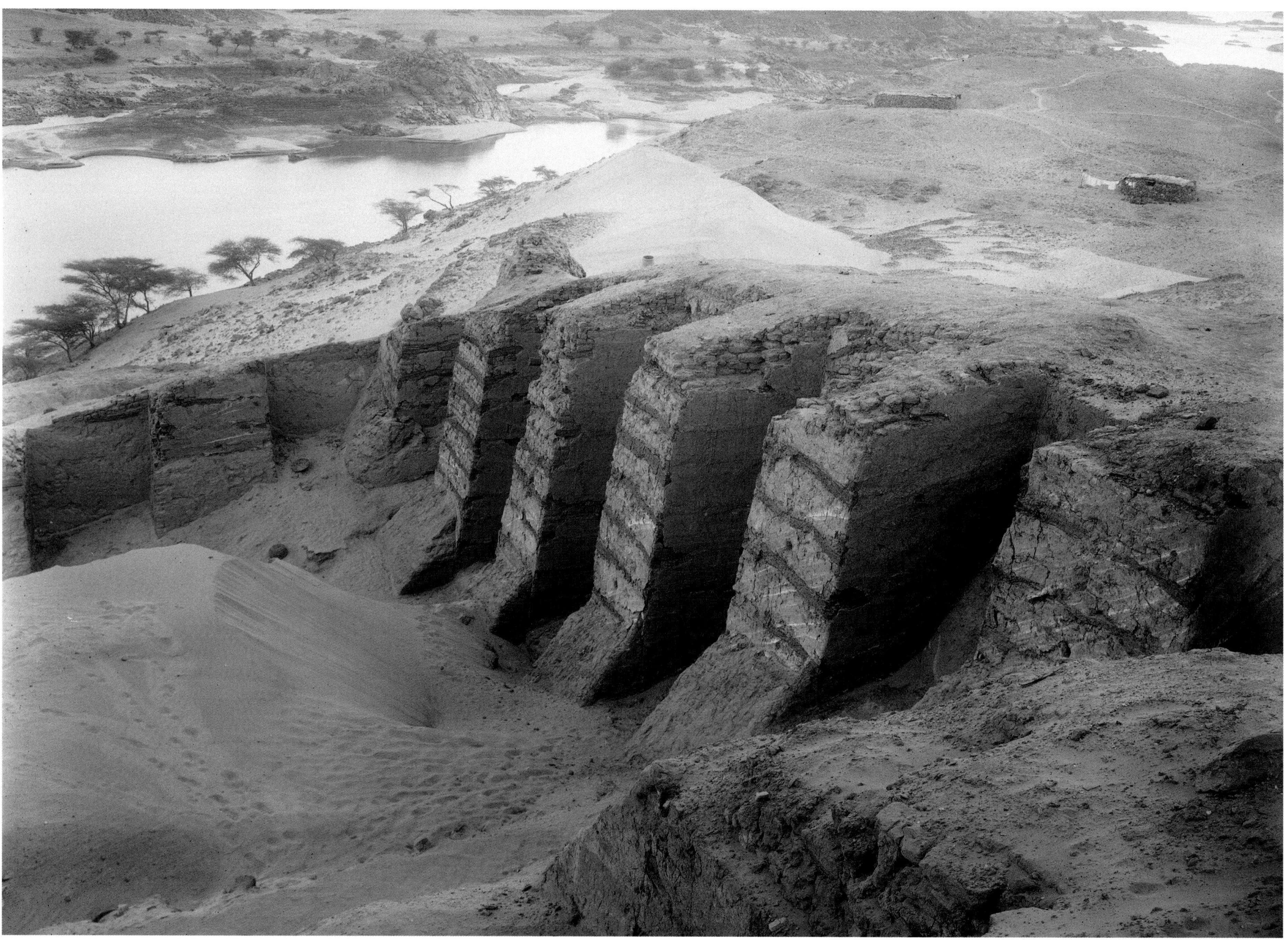

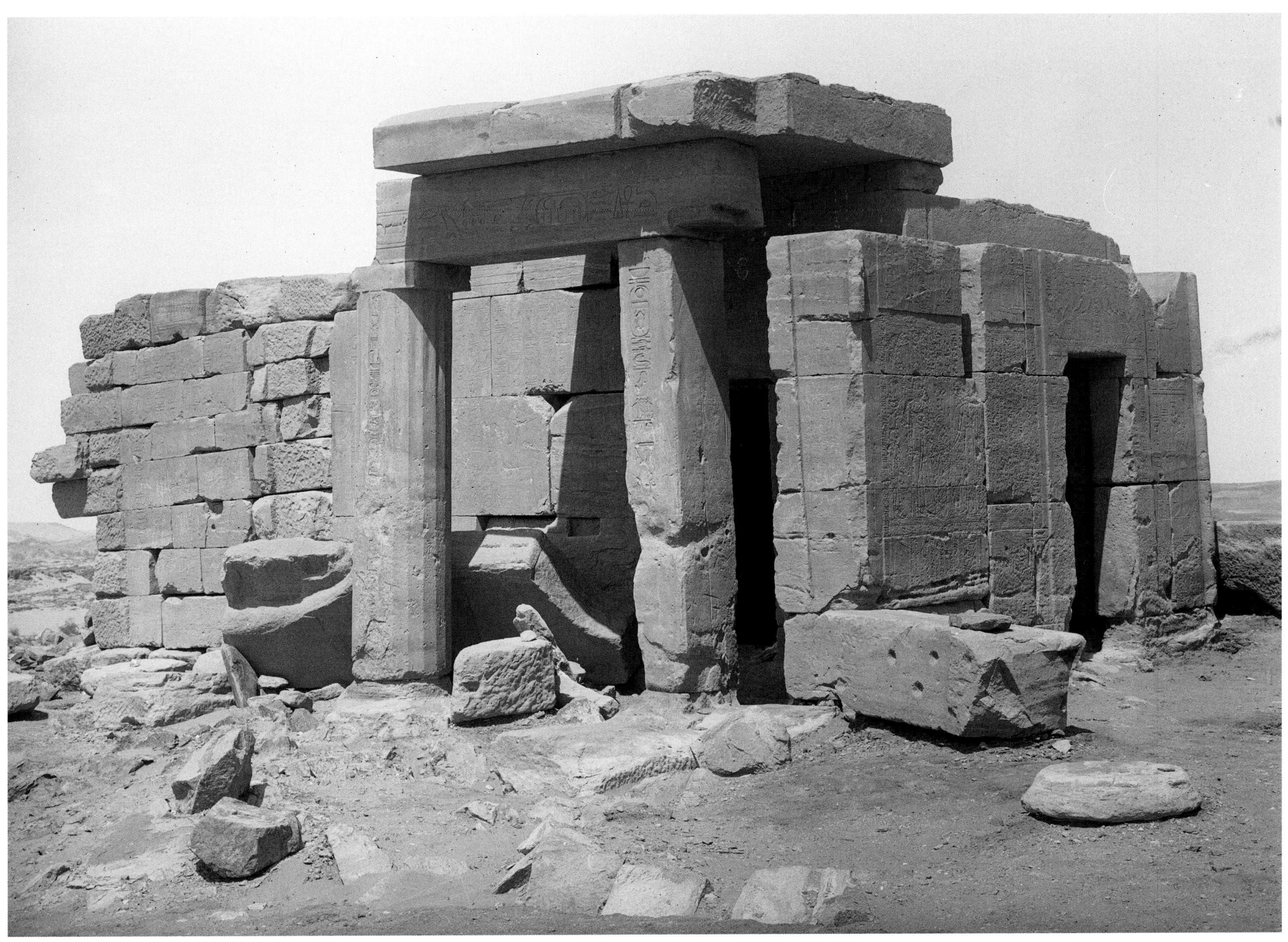

8

At Semna, a barrier of granitic rocks stretched across the Nile, over which the water rushed in torrents, forming the Second Cataract—a formidable barrier to navigation and a logical checkpoint for river traffic. [Mustapha Abu el-Hamd]

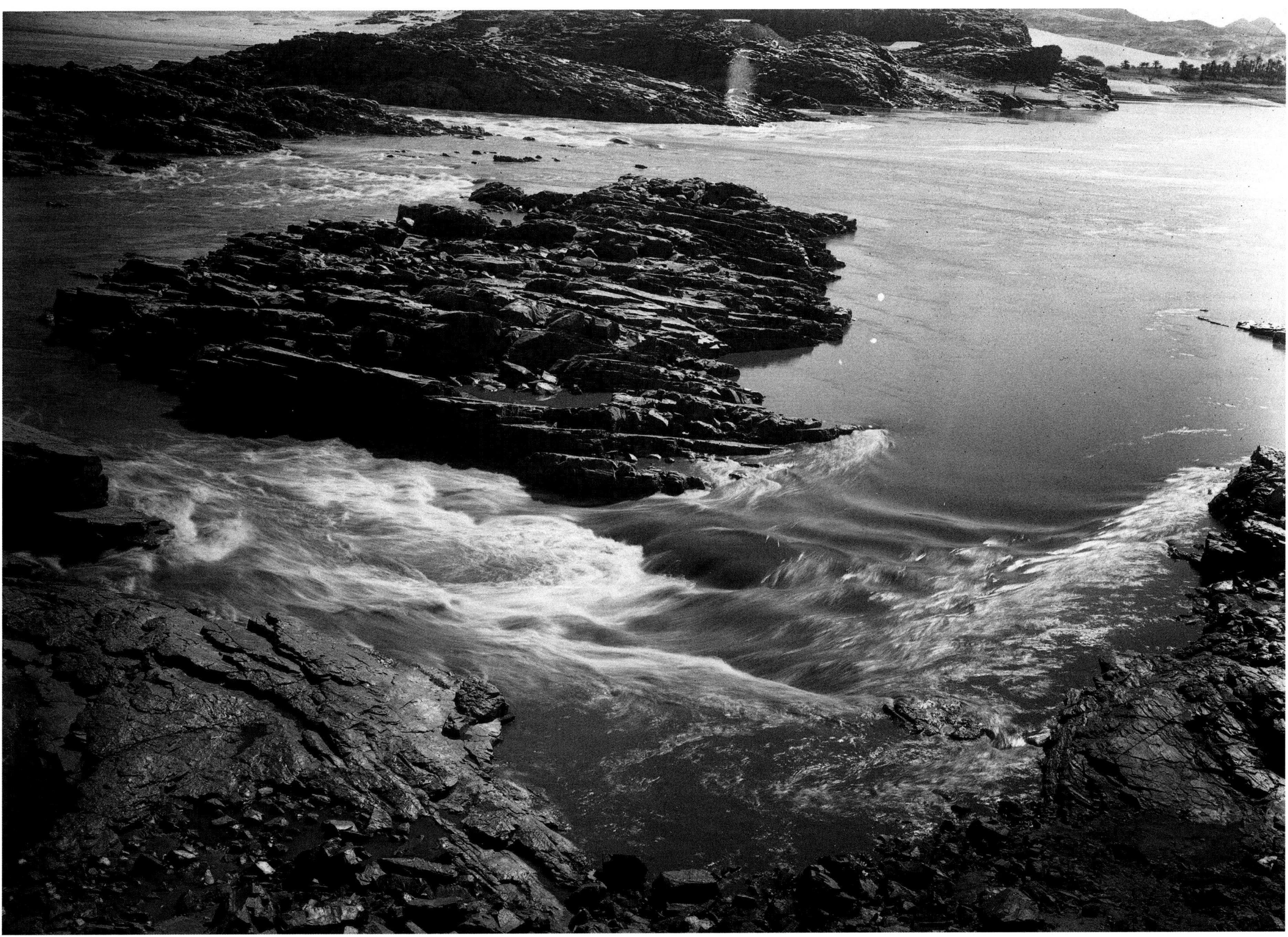

9

Boats could pass safely through the cataract only during flood season, when the Nile was high (normally July to October). Vessels laden with dates from northern Dongola Province sailed in fleets to help one another through the rapids. The return journey upstream to Sudan was the more difficult, as the boats had to be pulled against the current. In this photograph, taken in mid-November when the water had already begun to recede, the date fleet has gathered below the cataract before the season's last journey home. [Mustapha Abu el-Hamd]

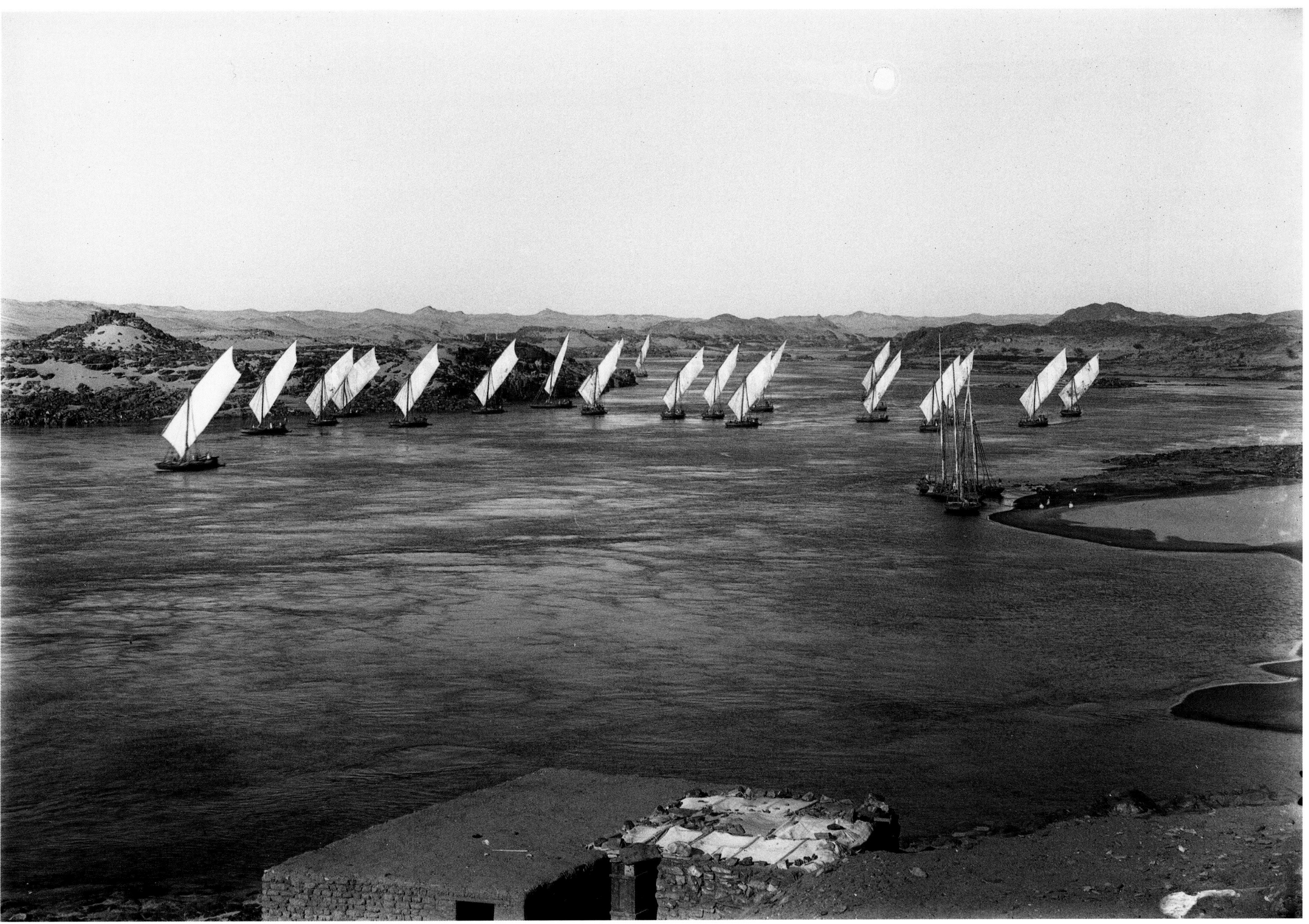

10

This view of Uronarti Island from the east bank of the Nile captures a picture-perfect
Nubian landscape. The Egyptian fortress is on the crest of the hill at the upper left.
[Mustapha Abu el-Hamd]

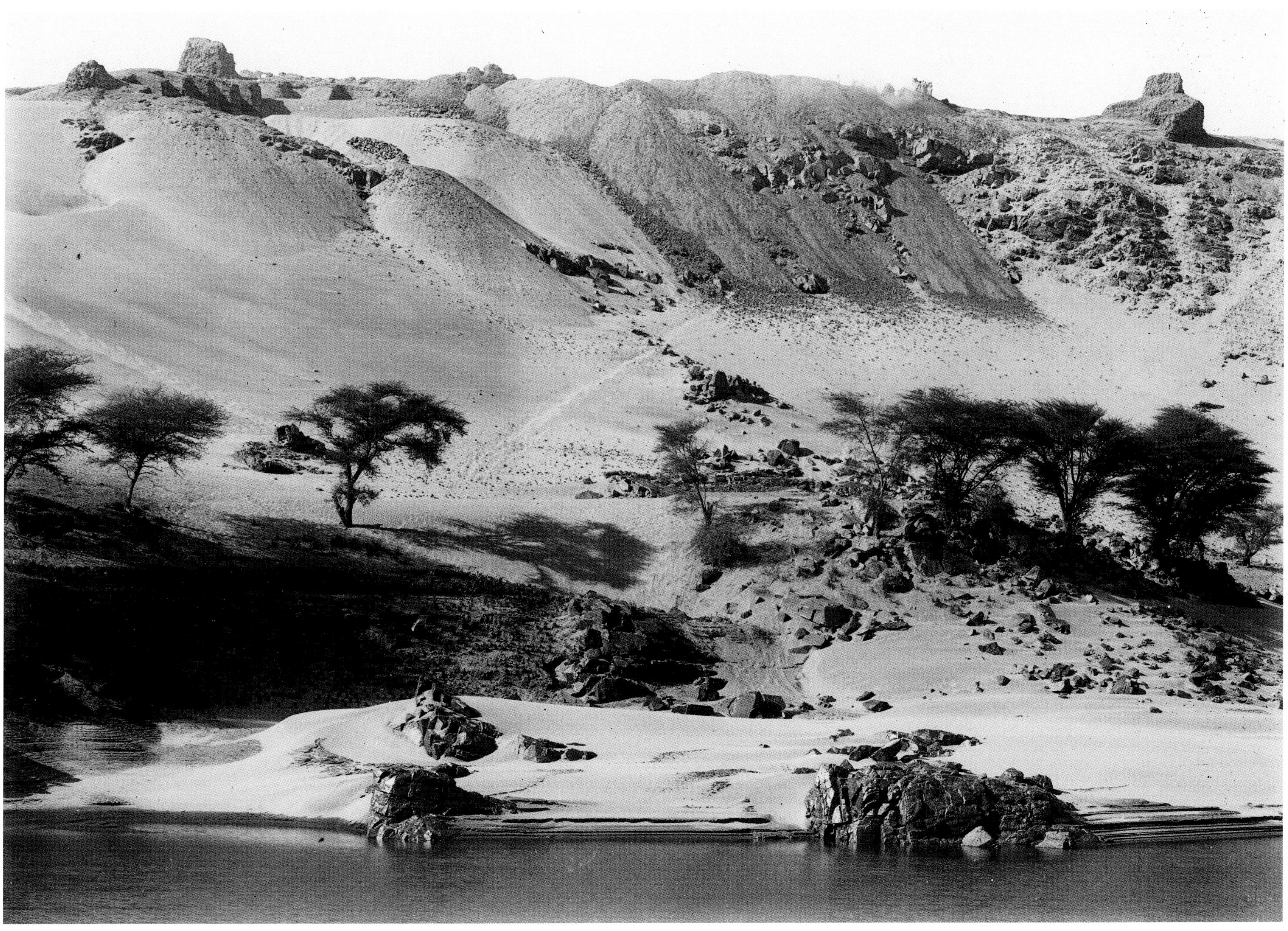

11

The site of Kerma is dominated by a temple structure called the Western Deffufa (from a Nubian word for a tall edifice of mudbrick), whose ruins stand over sixty feet high. Kerma was the capital of an independent Nubian kingdom that lasted for a thousand years and was a serious rival of Egypt during its peak, from 1700 to 1550 BC. [Mahmud Shadduf]

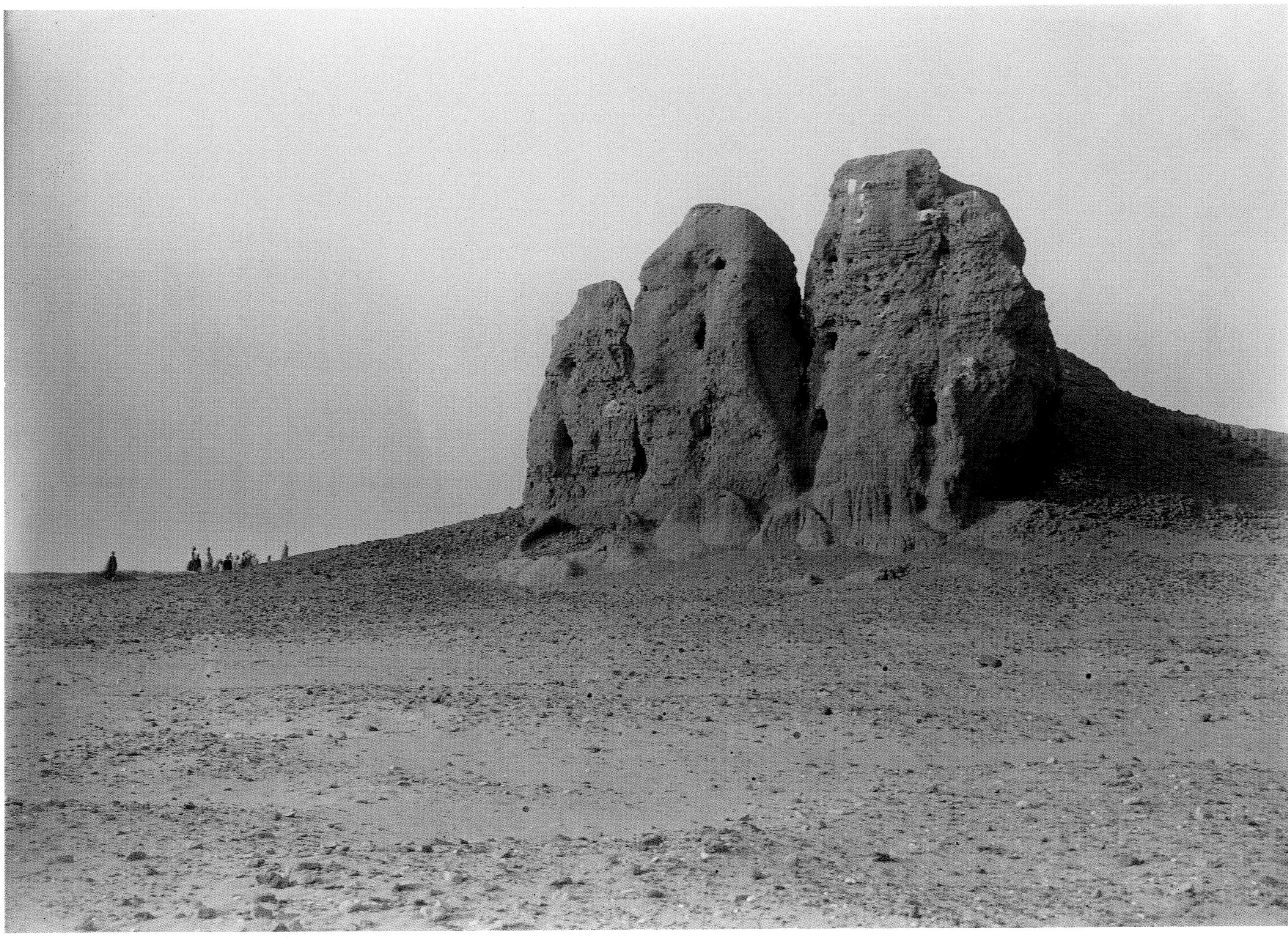

12

In the desert east of Kerma is a vast cemetery, with graves marked by low mounds of earth (or tumuli) encircled by rings of stones. The tumulus graves look like flying saucers buried in the sand. [Mohammedani Ibrahim Ibrahim]

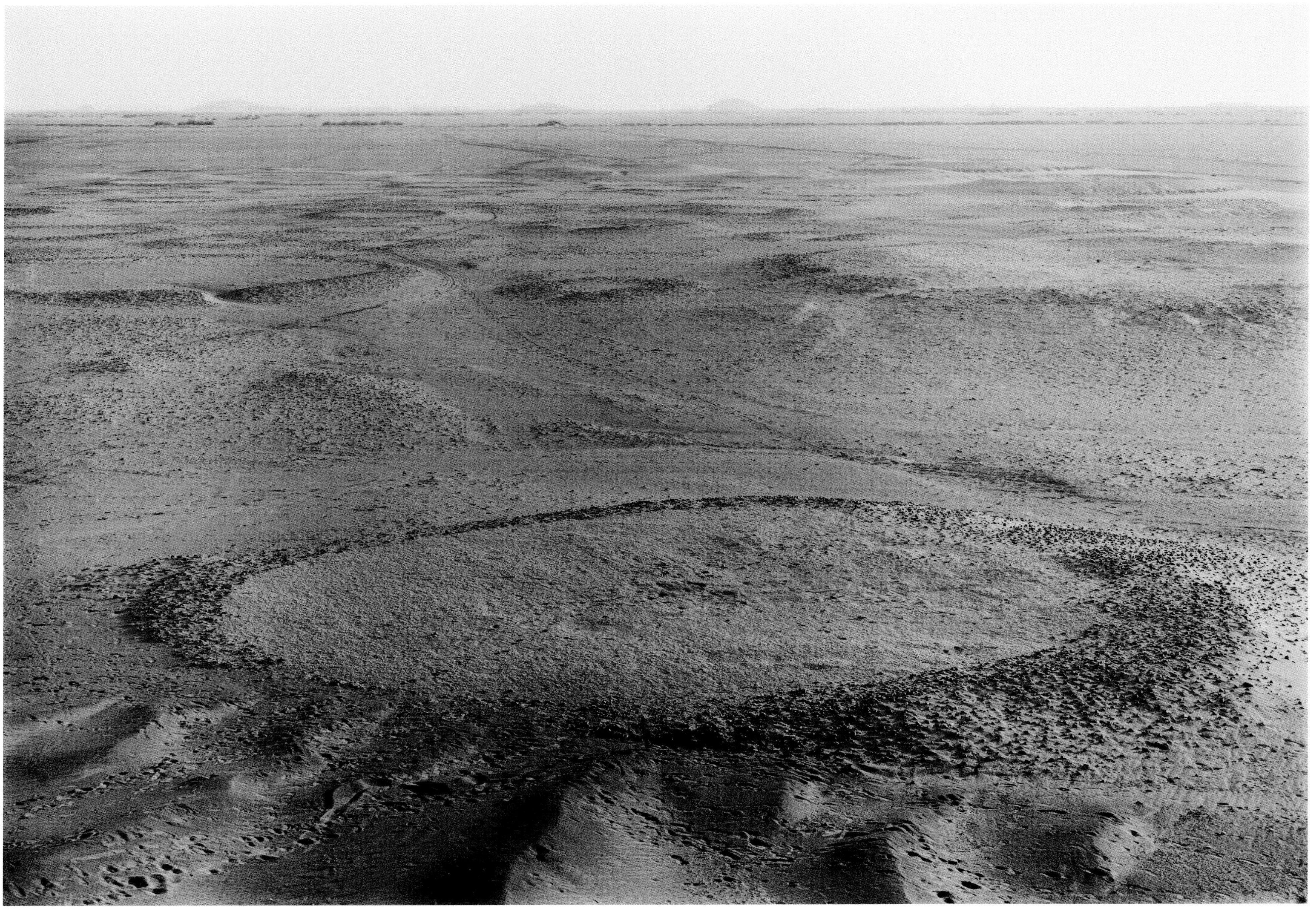

13

The largest tumuli belonged to the kings of Kerma and measured up to three hundred feet (ninety
meters) across. Inside each was a honeycomb of mudbrick retaining walls defining chambers
filled with sand that helped support the domed shape. The tall structure in the background, known
as the Eastern Deffufa, probably served as a funerary chapel. [Mohammedani Ibrahim Ibrahim]

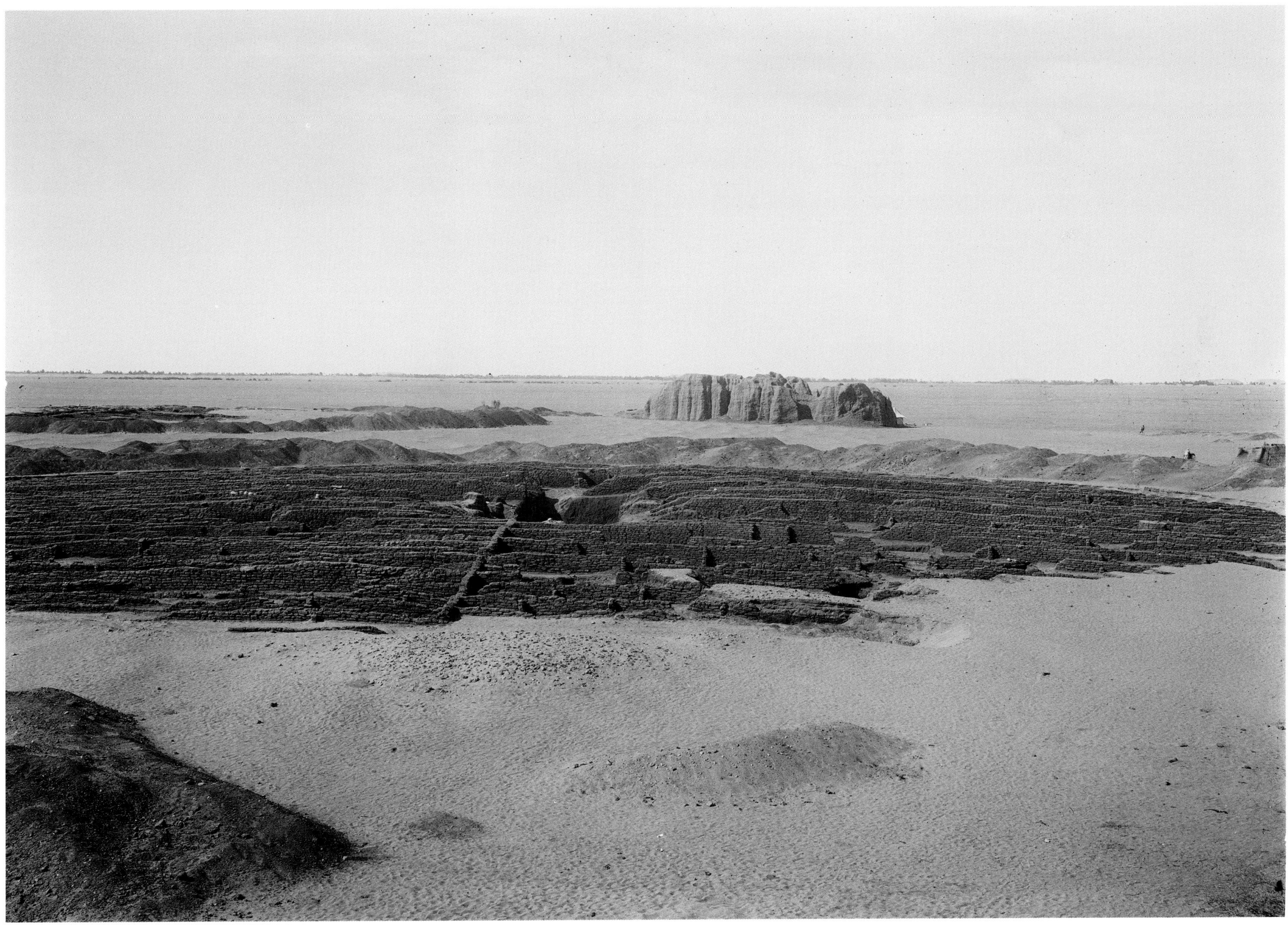

14

At Nuri, by the Fourth Cataract of the Nile, is the main royal cemetery of the Napatan Period (750–300 BC). Here, from 1916 to 1918, Reisner identified the pyramids of twenty-two kings and fifty-three queens of ancient Sudan, all but a handful of whom were previously unknown to scholarship. Smaller and rising at a steeper angle than Egyptian royal pyramids, they had been robbed of the smooth outer casing stones that preserved their shapes and presented wild and irregular contours. [Mohammedani Ibrahim Ibrahim]

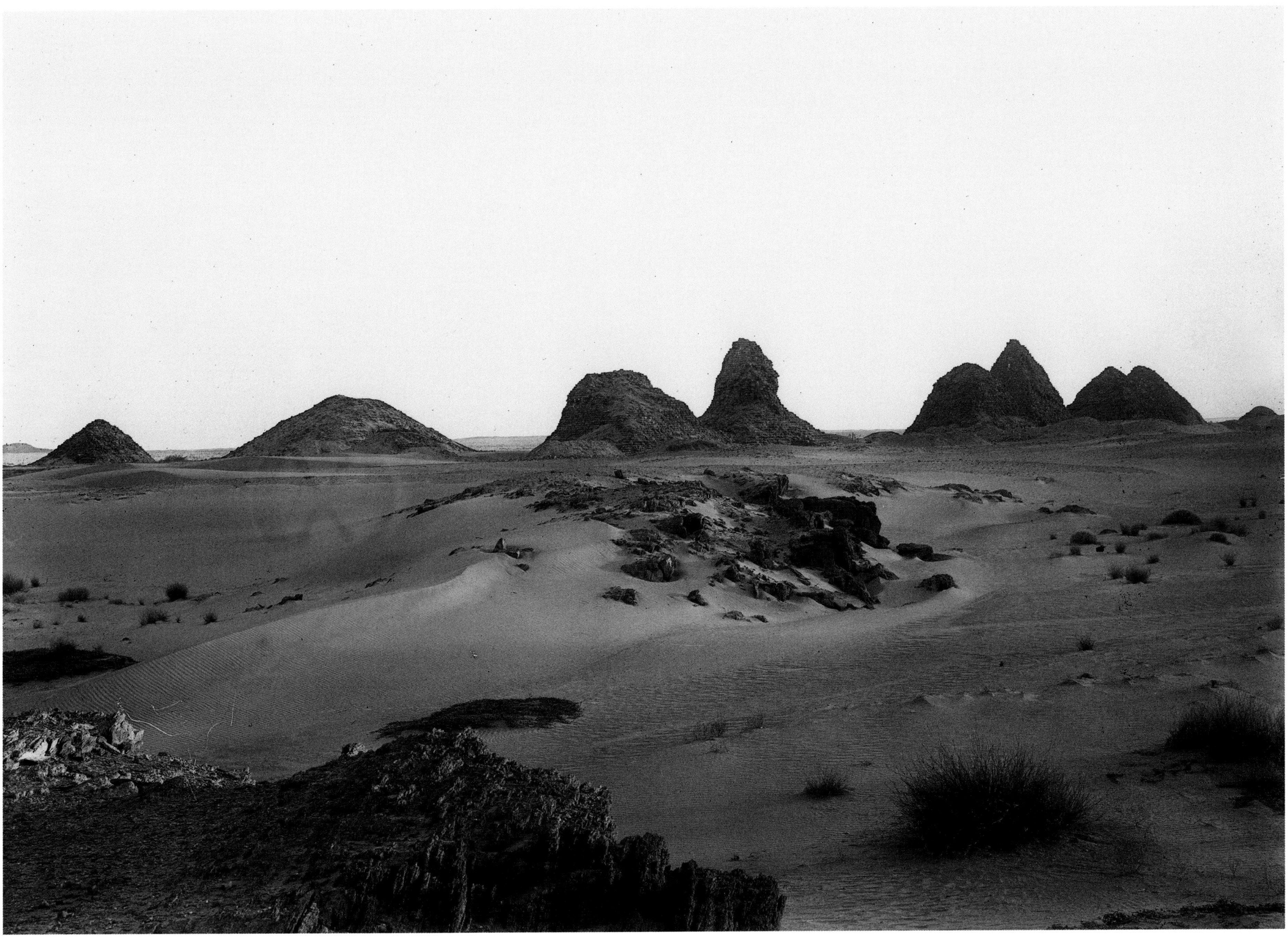

15

This view of the Nuri cemetery before excavation presents an aspect of utmost desolation.
[Mohammedani Ibrahim Ibrahim]

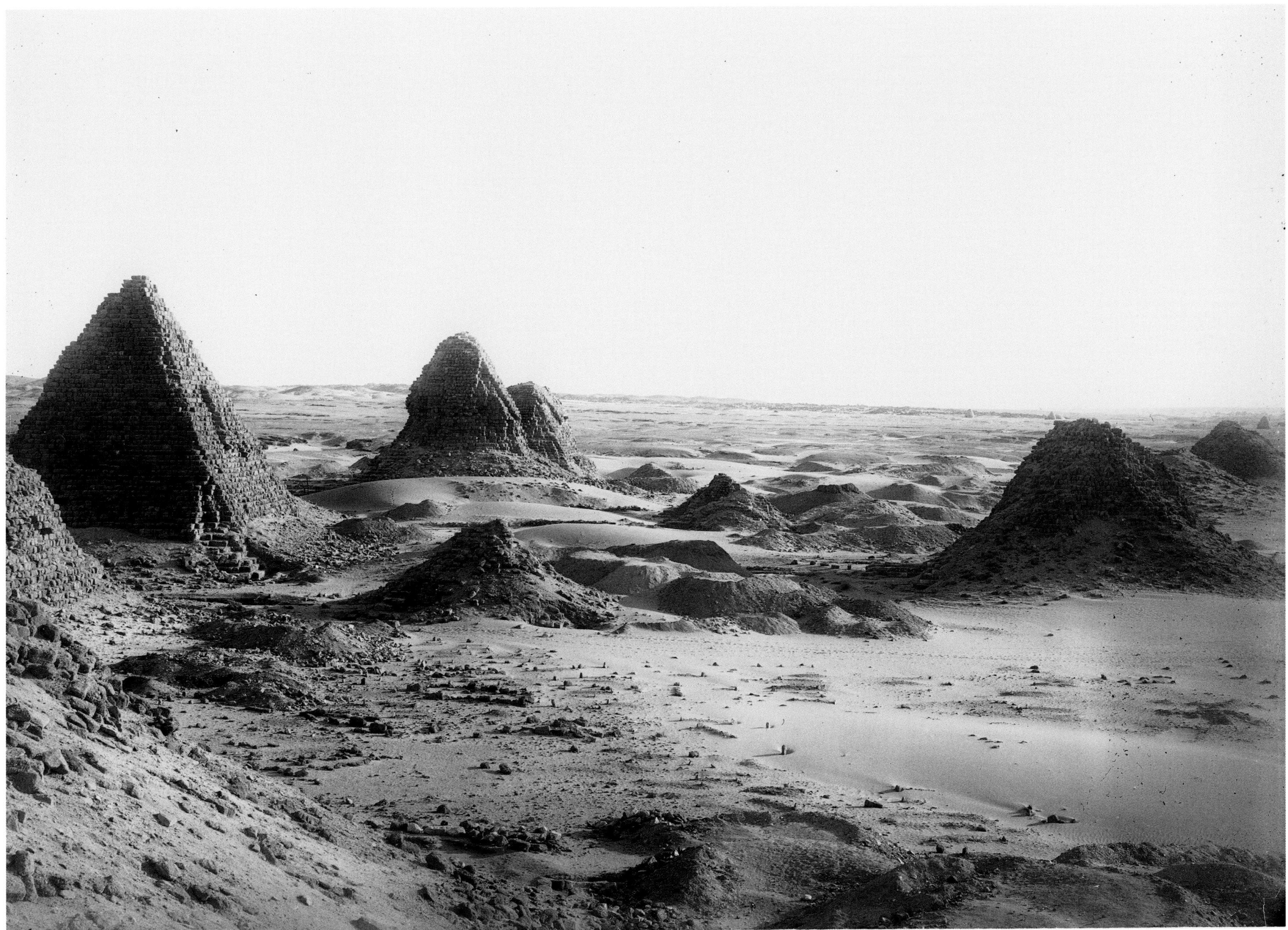

16

In 1920 the expedition moved its operations farther south to Meroe, where it excavated three pyramid cemeteries on the high desert east of the ancient city. This photograph, taken before excavation, is of the North Cemetery at Begrawiya, where Reisner's team identified the tombs of thirty kings, eight reigning queens, and two princes of the Meroitic Period (300 BC–AD 350). [Mohammedani Ibrahim Ibrahim]

17 [overleaf]

A closer view of the cemetery shows the chapels in front of the pyramids, built in the form of small temples with pylon gateways that are decorated with images of the ruler smiting his enemies. [Mohammedani Ibrahim Ibrahim]

18 [overleaf]

This cluster of pyramids in the desert west of Gebel Barkal was the first pyramid cemetery excavated by the Harvard-MFA expedition. The pyramids date from the third to the first century BC. [Mohammedani Ibrahim Ibrahim]

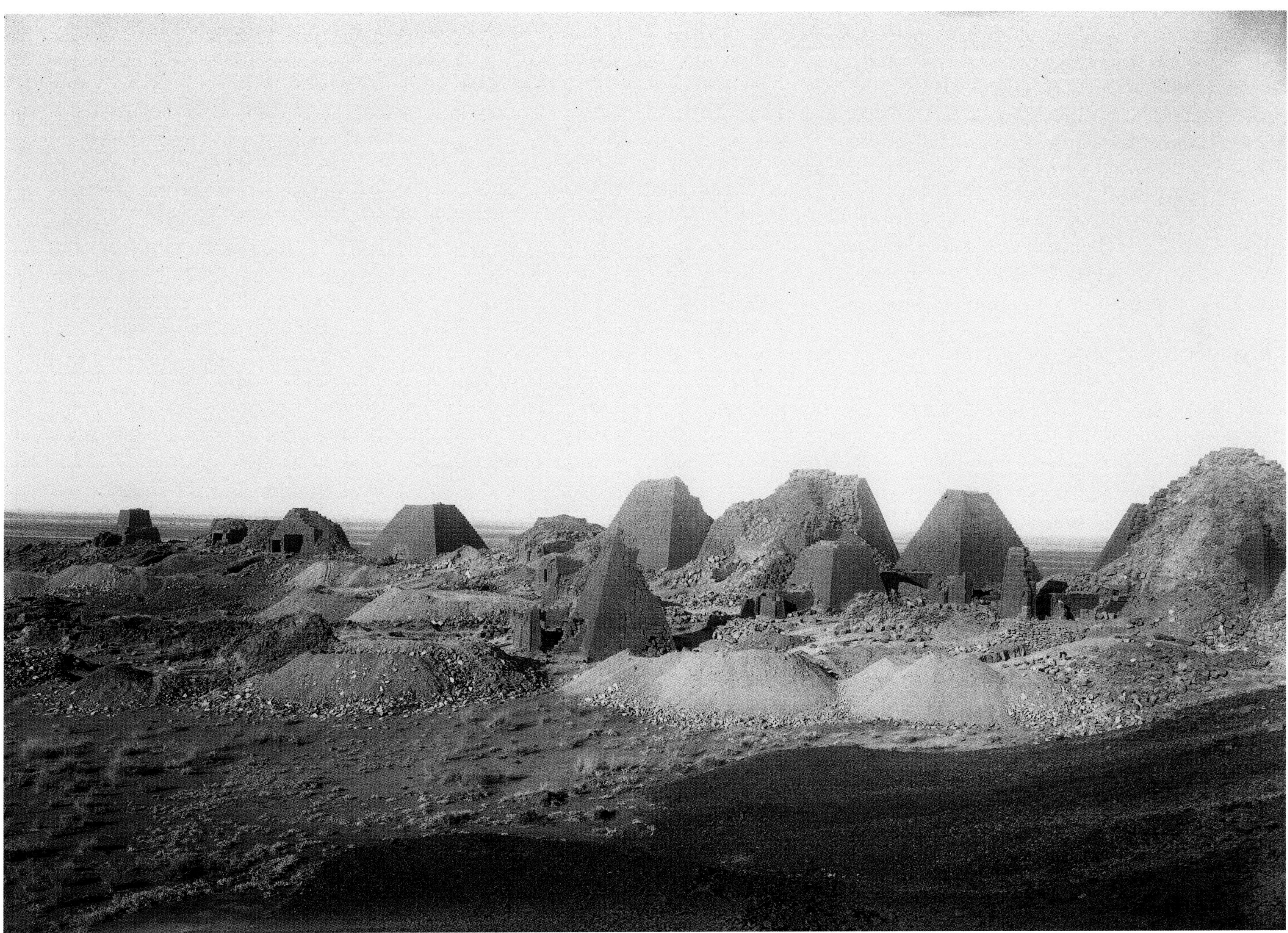

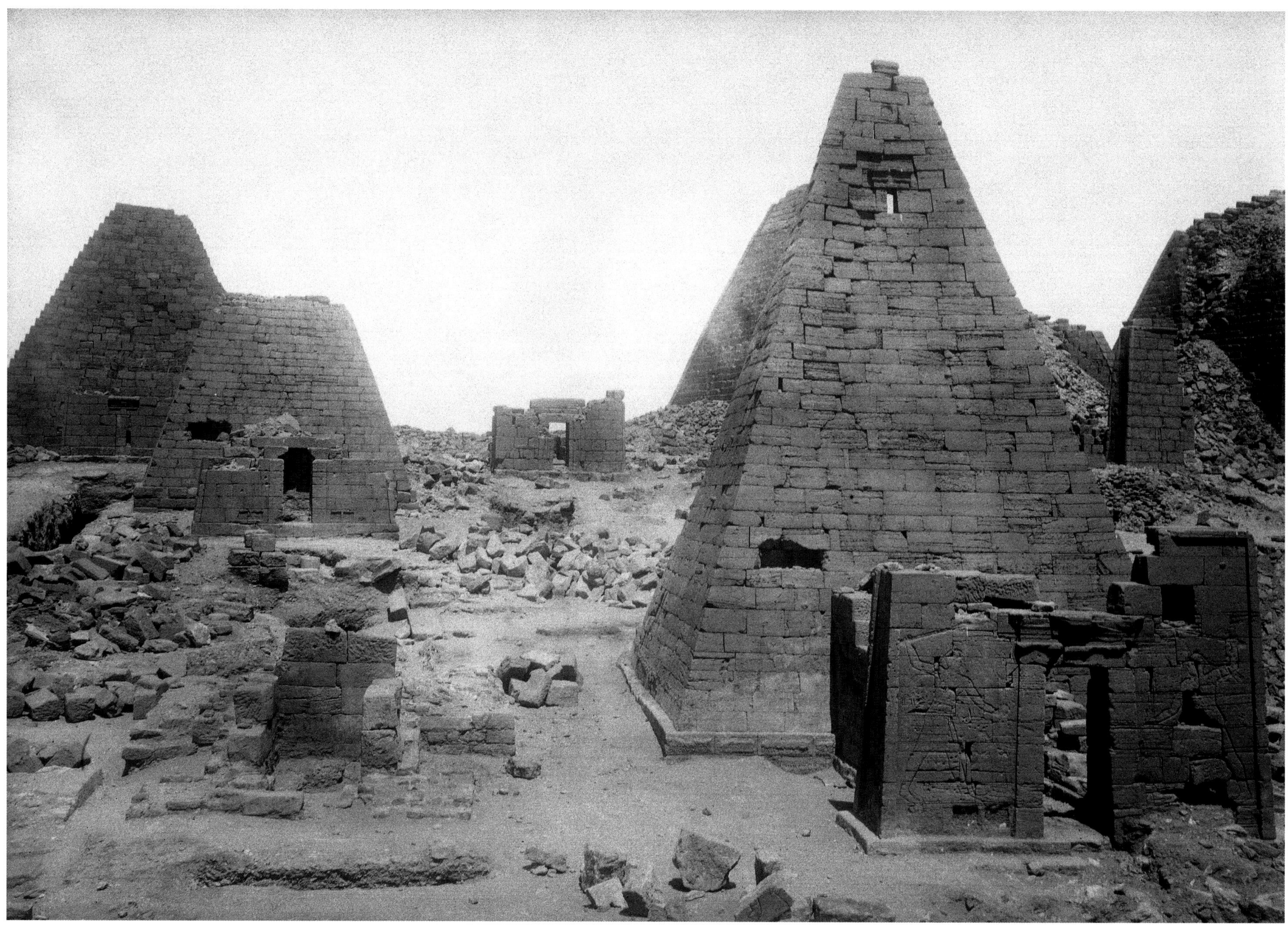

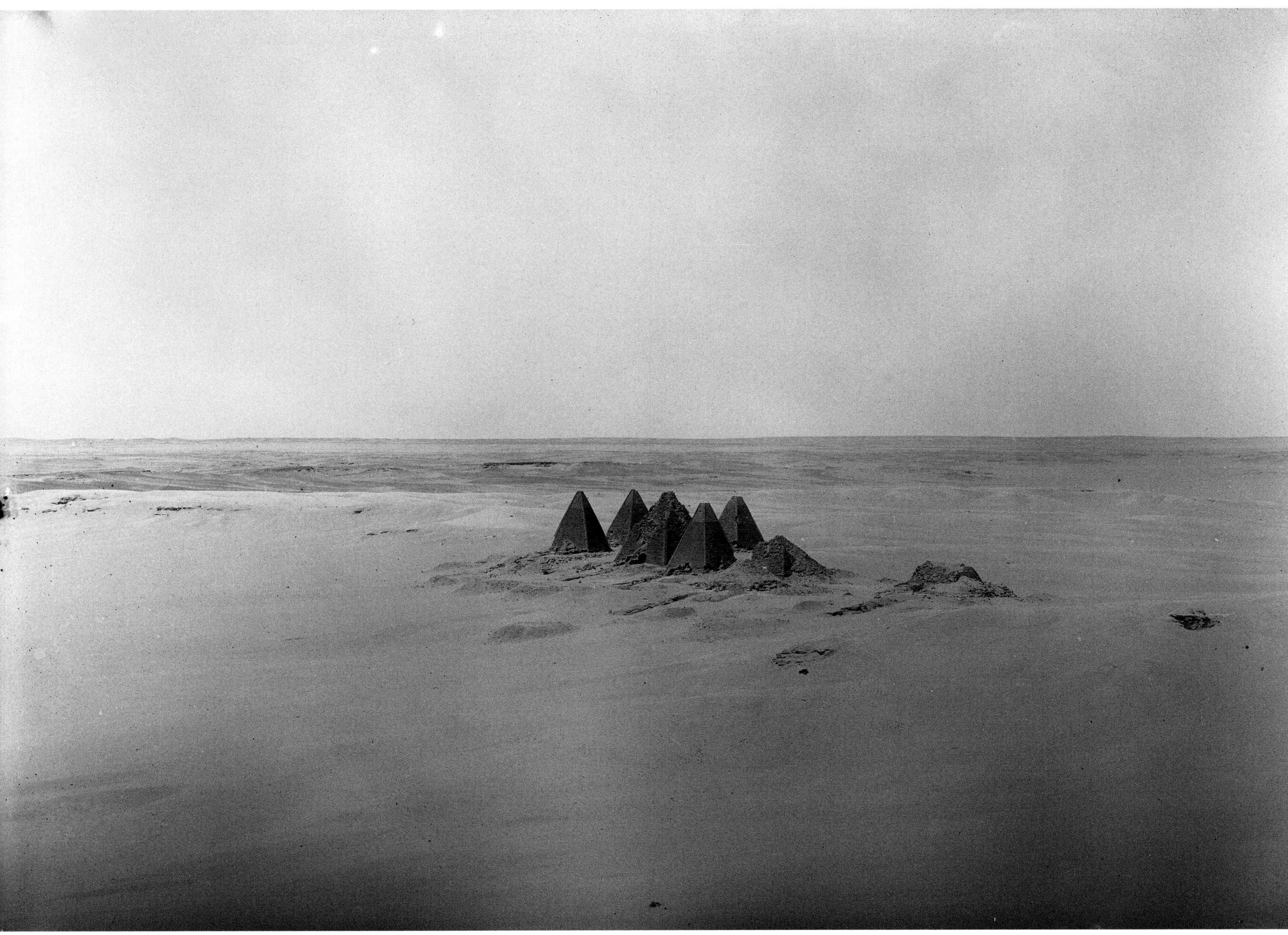

19

On the very first day of work at the Barkal pyramids (January 23, 1916), Reisner uncovered
the secret of the burial chambers that had eluded previous researchers. The underground
chambers were not directly connected to the pyramids above them. Rather, they were accessed
by a stairway whose concealed entrance was located outside, in front of the chapel on
the east side of the pyramid. In five days the expedition had cleared the burial chambers of
twenty-five pyramids. [Mohammedani Ibrahim Ibrahim]

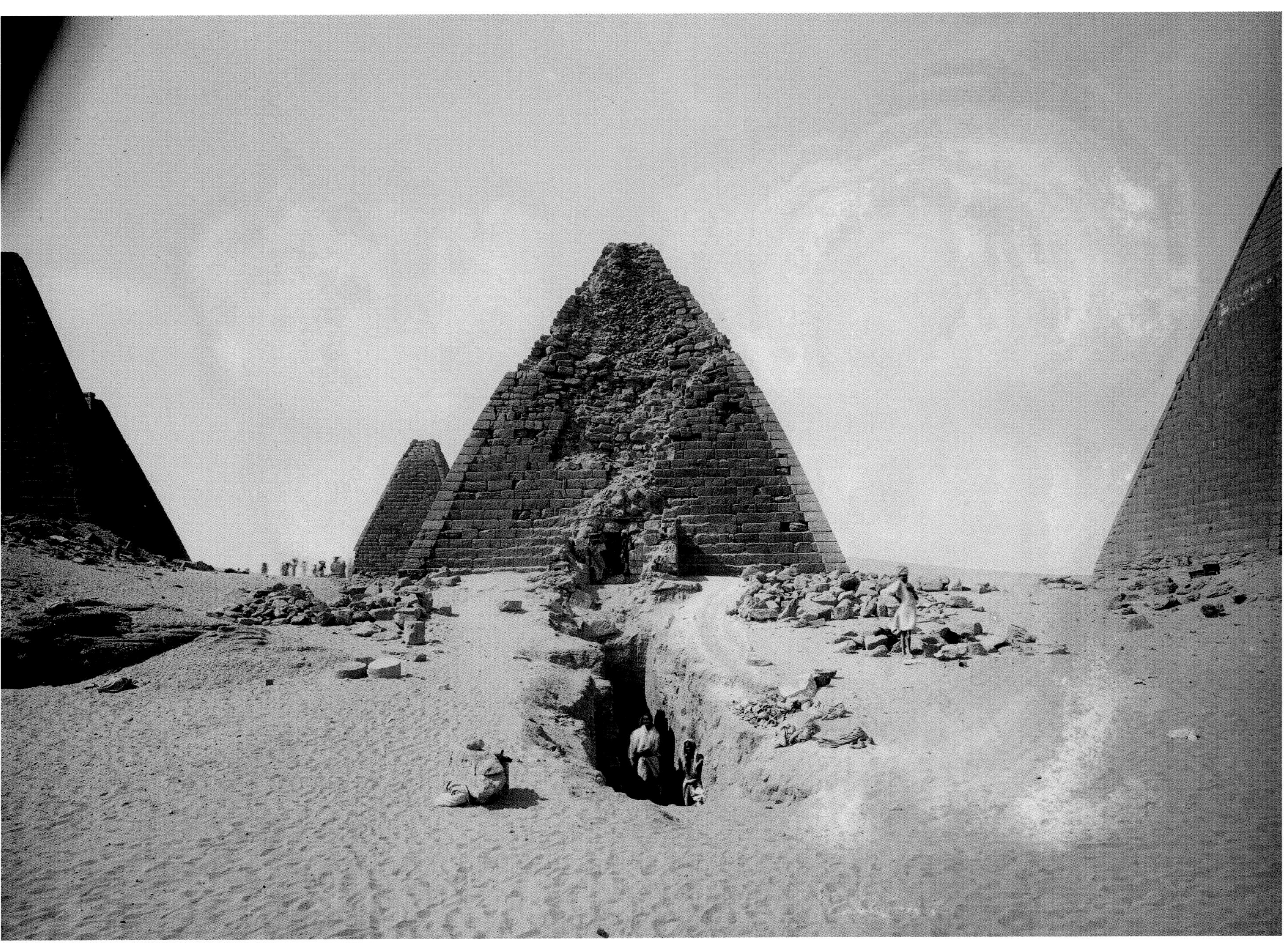

20

A fly in the ointment. Whereas small objects could be photographed in the controlled environment of a studio, excavations in progress such as at the Nuri pyramids could be photographed only onsite. With the difficulties of working in heat, wind, and sand, it is remarkable that more mishaps like this one—where an insect caught in the emulsion has been immortalized like a fossil in amber—did not occur. [Mohammedani Ibrahim Ibrahim]

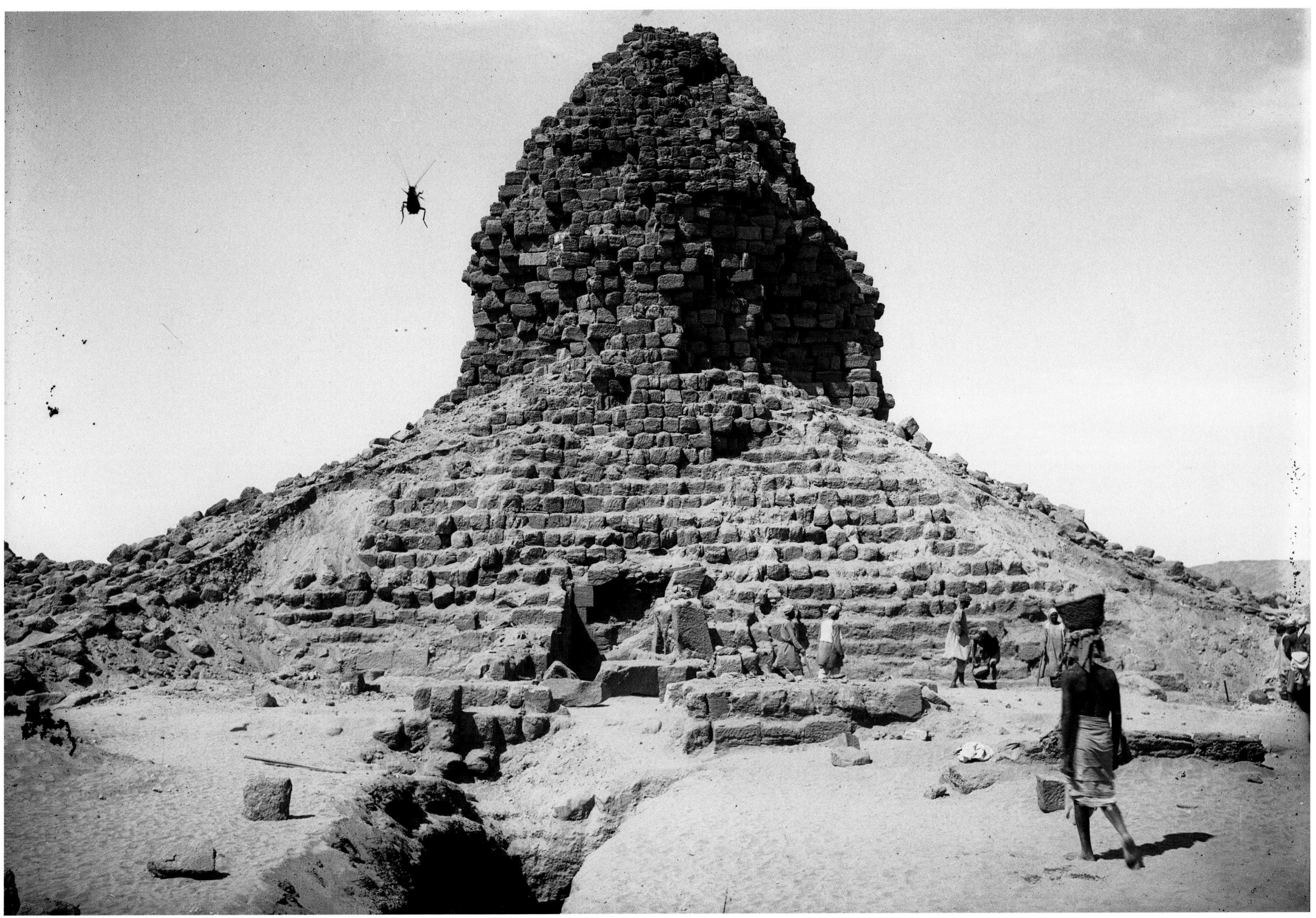

21

In addition to the trained Egyptian excavators, the expedition employed hundreds of local Sudanese
to do the heavy work of clearing out debris and carrying it away. Here, a group of basket carriers,
having just emerged from the stairway, pauses before the camera. [Mohammedani Ibrahim Ibrahim]

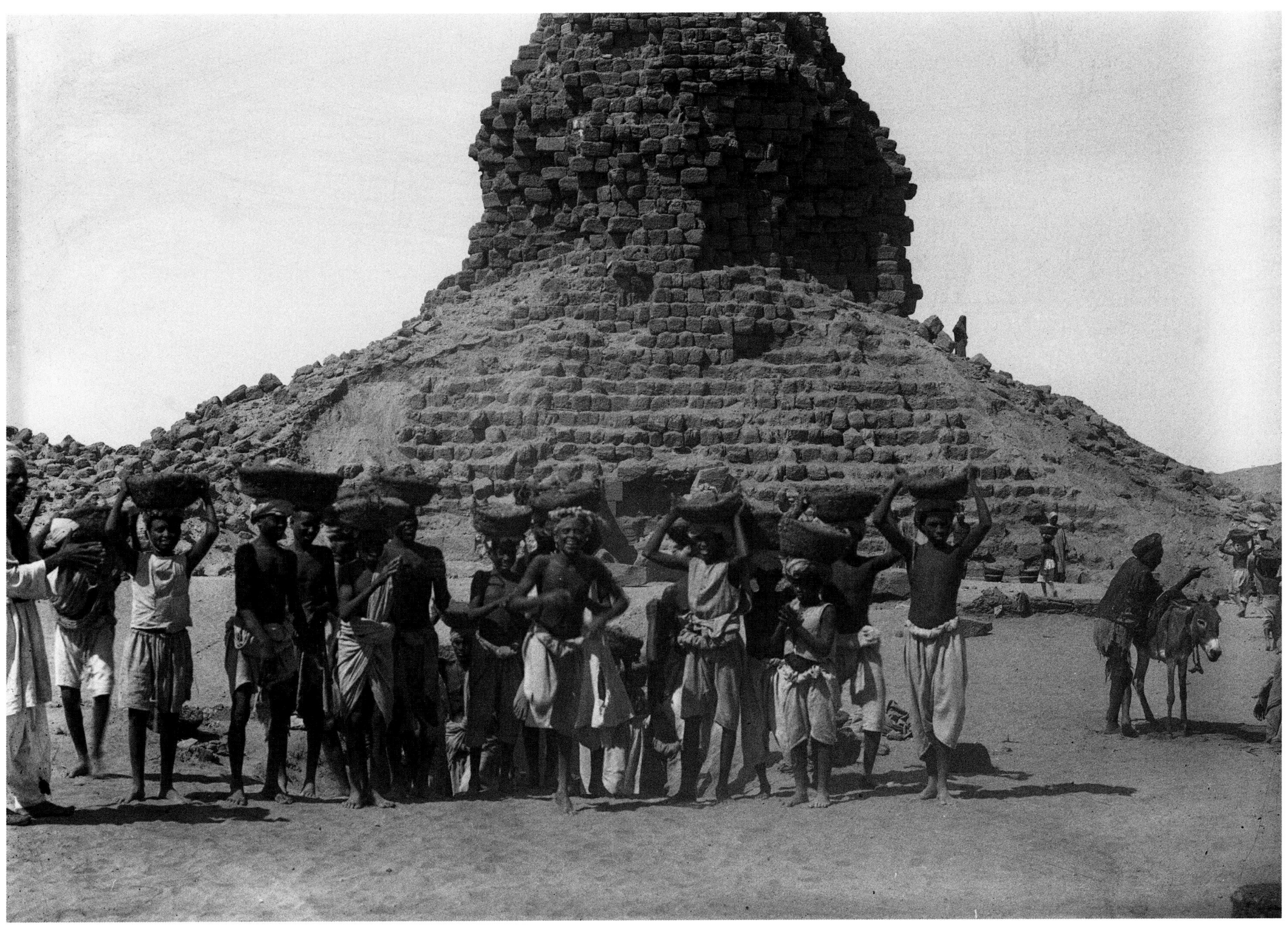

22

This classically balanced composition places the pyramid and its stairway in the center, a group of workers holding baskets in the left foreground, and another group of workers farther back on the right. Only those in the group on the left seem aware of the camera. [Mohammedani Ibrahim Ibrahim]

23 [overleaf]

Looking up the stairway of a pyramid at Gebel Barkal into glaring sunlight. [Mohammedani Ibrahim Ibrahim]

24 [overleaf]

A doorway at the foot of the entrance stair in a queen's pyramid at Nuri. [Mohammedani Ibrahim Ibrahim]

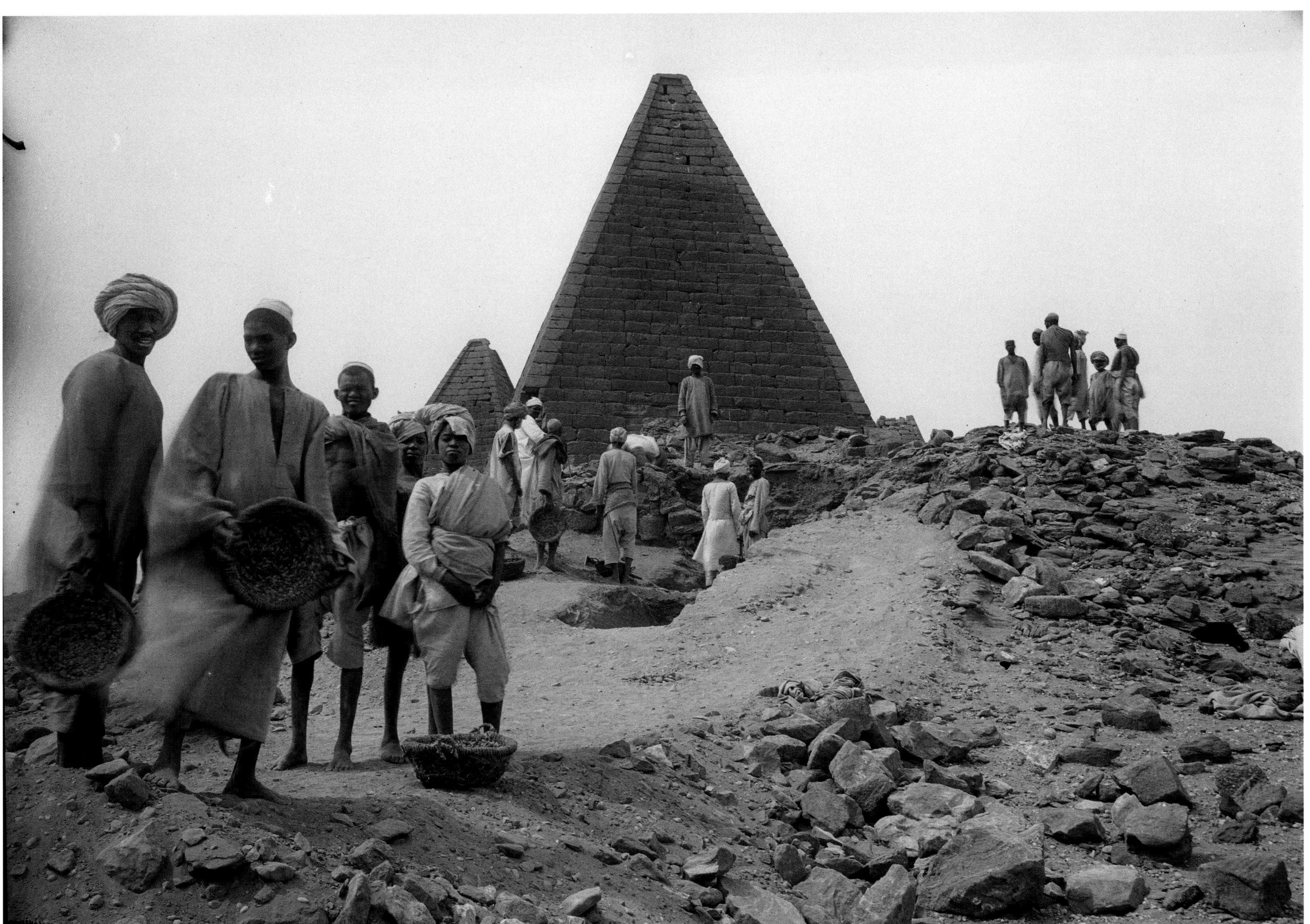

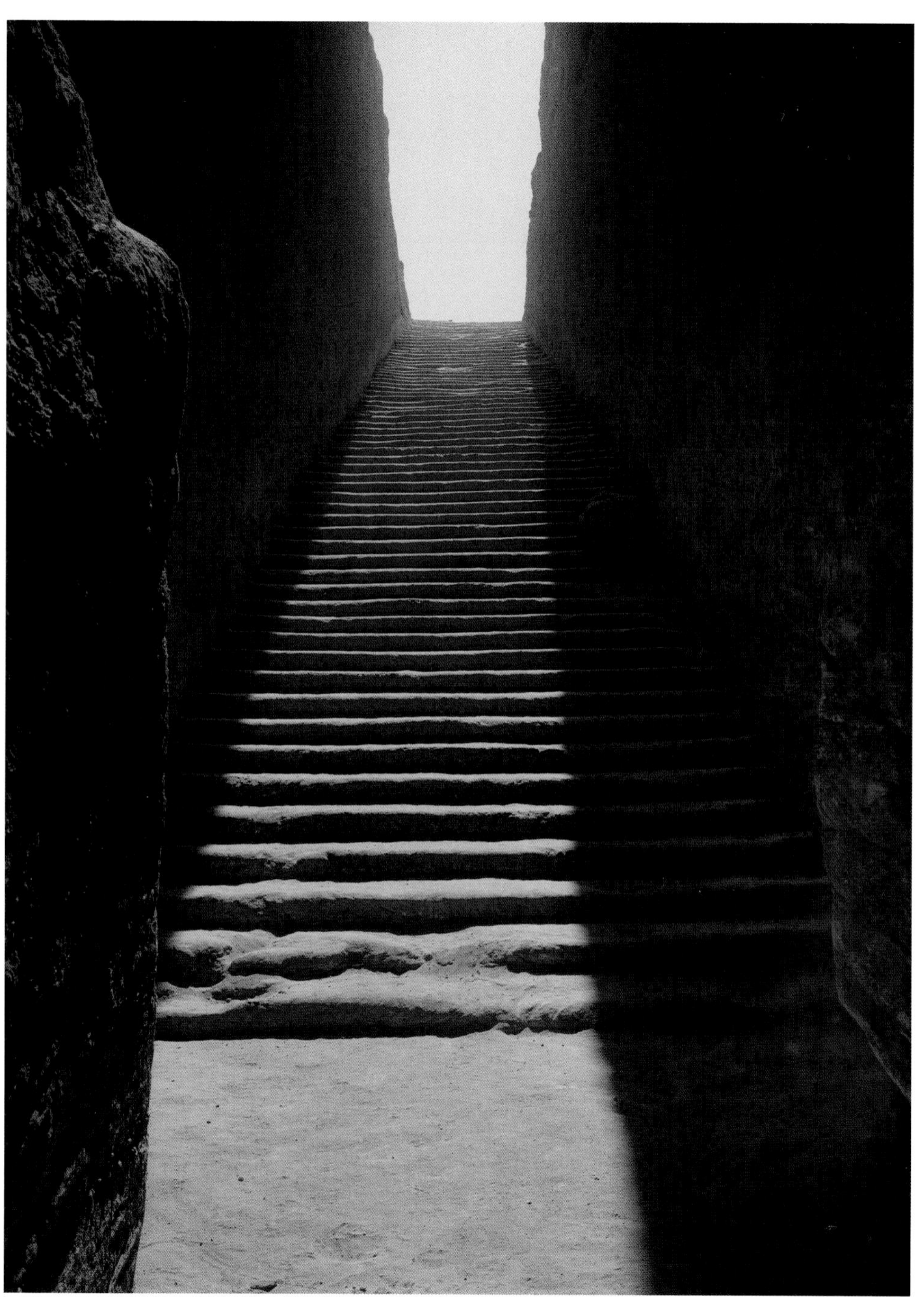

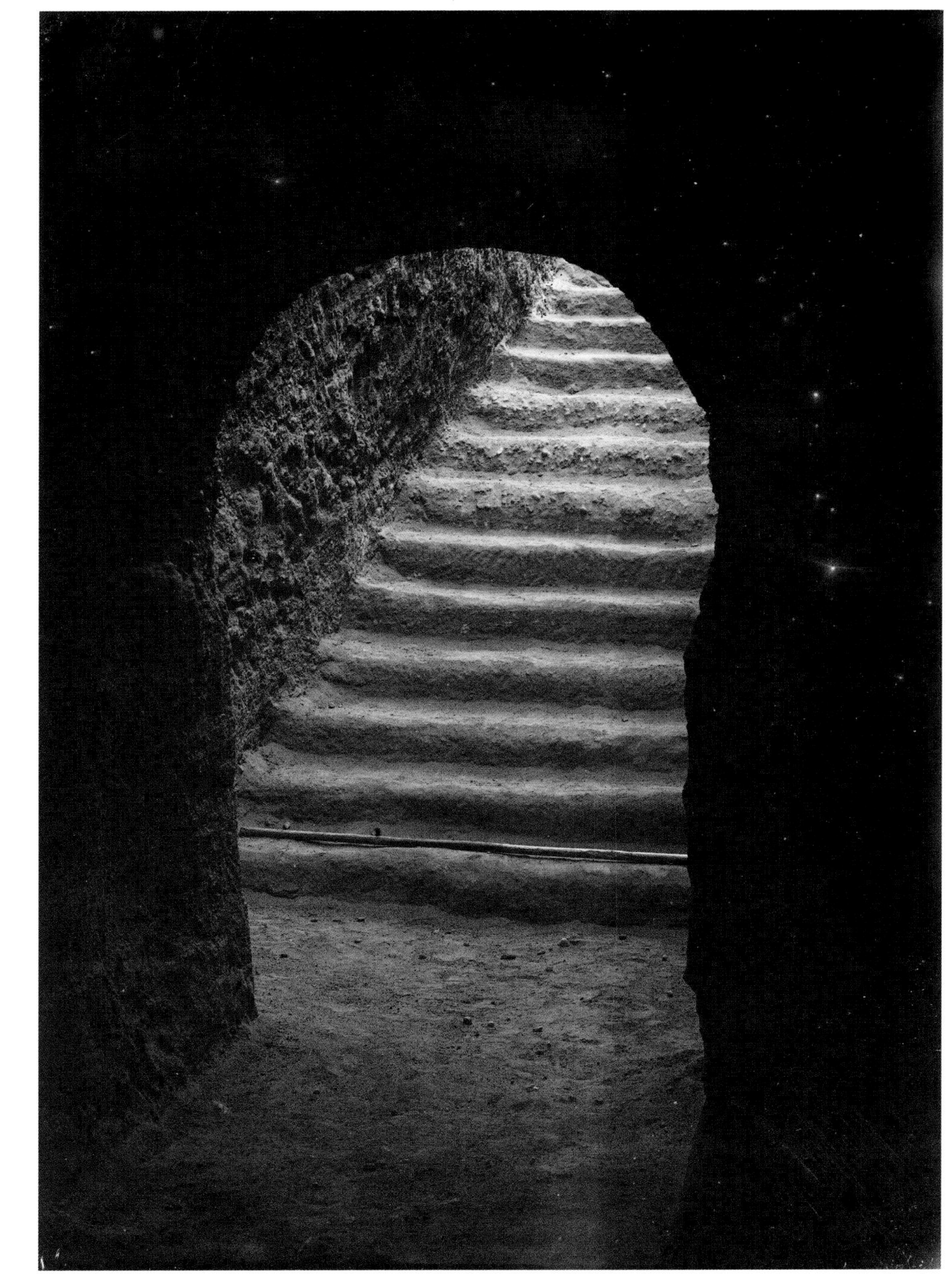

25

The painted burial chamber of King Tanwetamani at el-Kurru, looking toward the stairway.
Stars cover the vaulted ceiling and funerary deities flank the doorway, while above the arch the
sun god traverses the sky in his boat as sacred baboons with arms uplifted jabber his praises.
[Mahmud Shadduf]

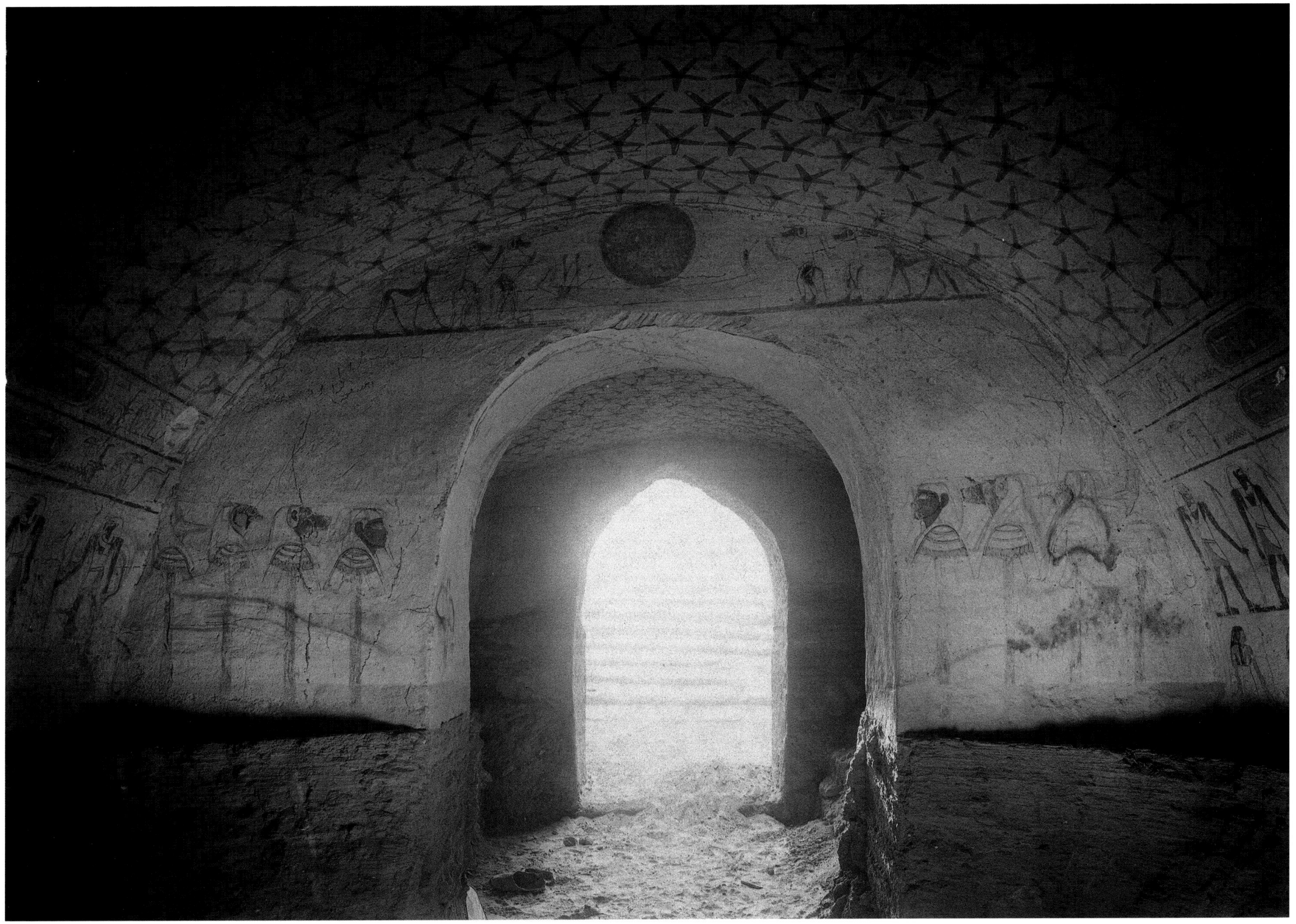

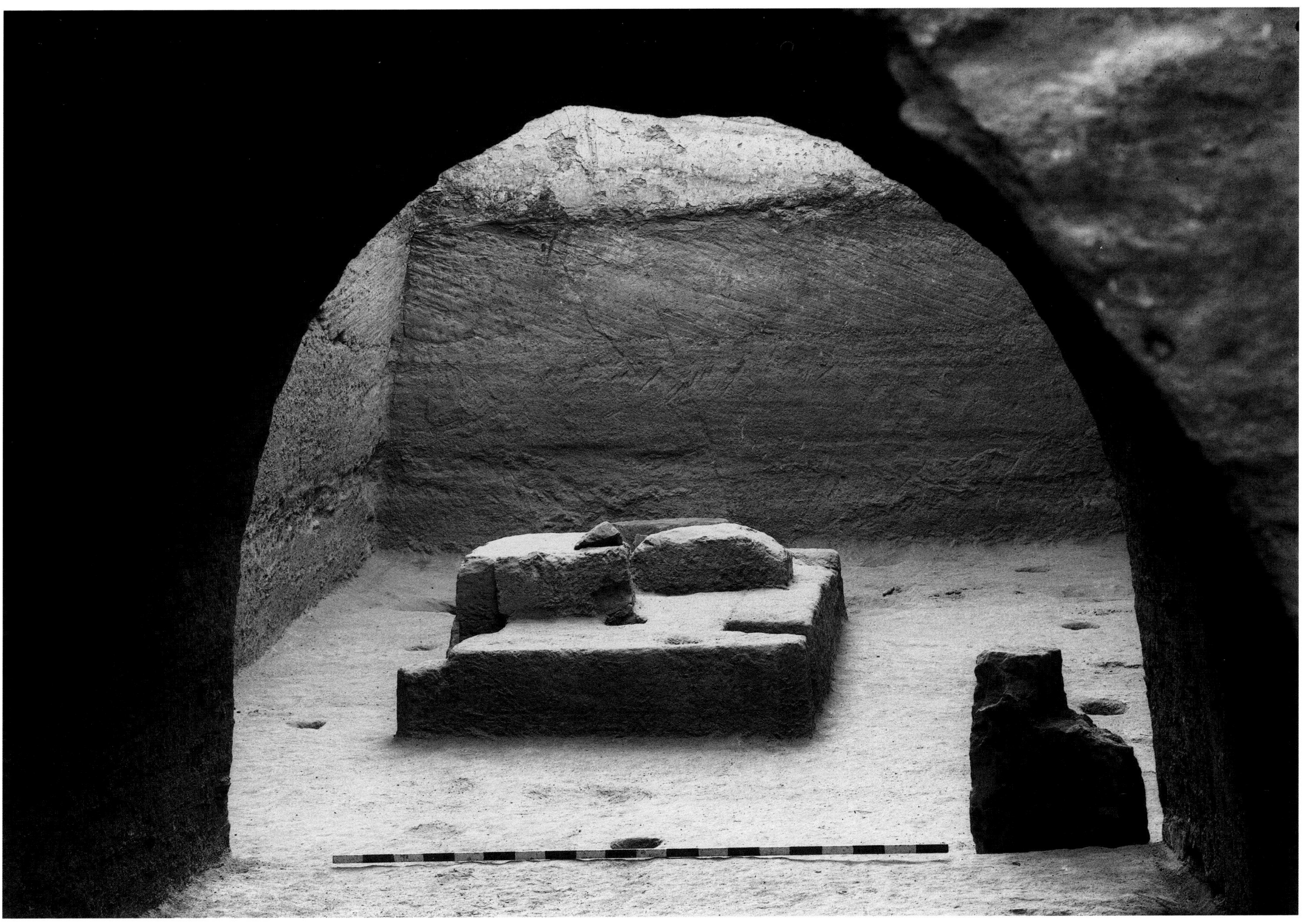

27

In the burial apartments below the pyramid of King Taharqa at Nuri, a worker (identified in the records only as "B. Mahmud") stands in the passage between two rooms, his right arm portentously raised. Although the walls of the burial chambers are covered with hieroglyphic inscriptions, the passageway is bare. What is he pointing at? [Mahmud Shadduf]

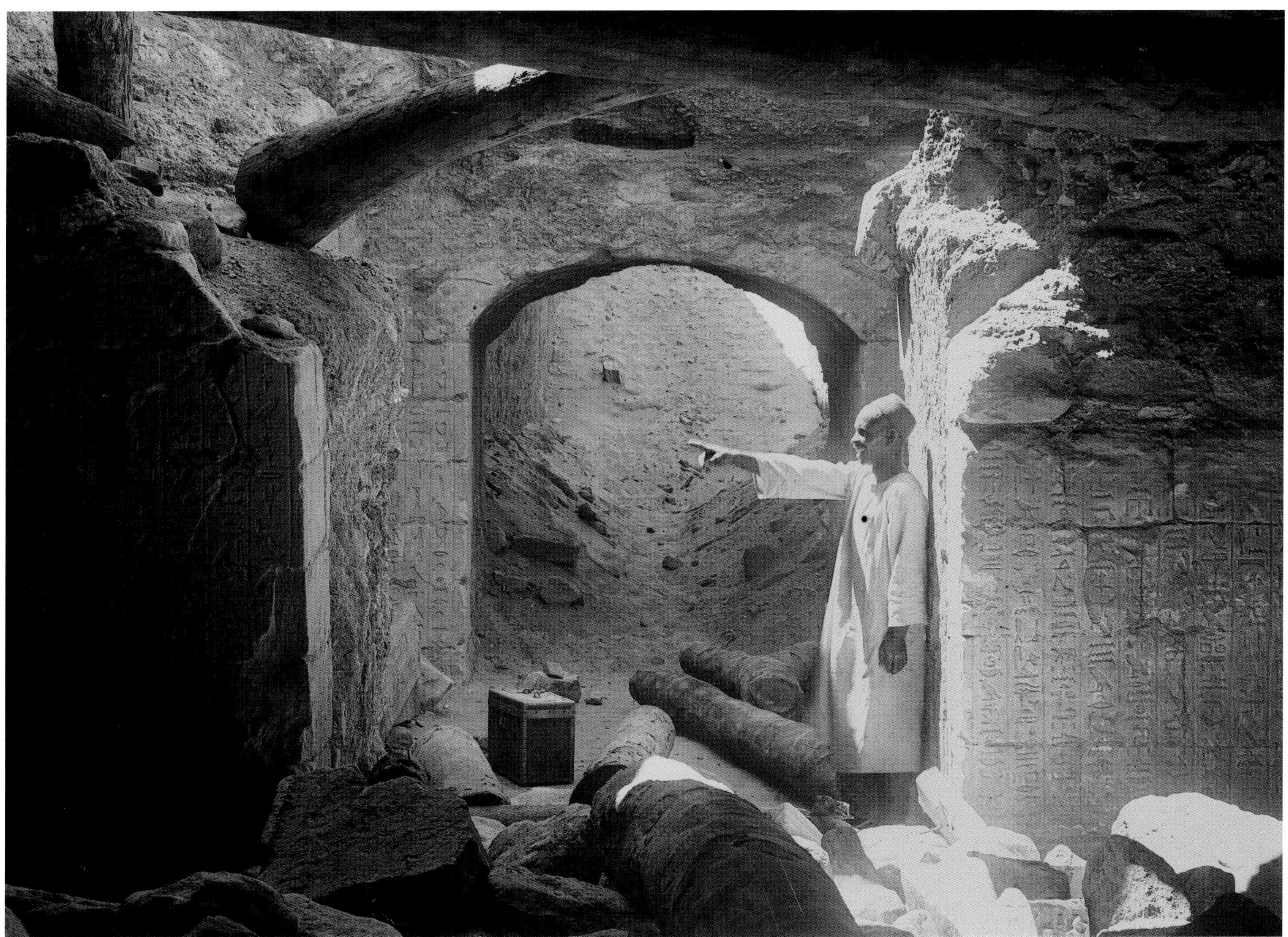

28

All of the tombs at Nuri had been plundered long ago; however, the tomb of Aspelta preserved more treasure than most. Reisner attributed this to the roof's having collapsed in antiquity. In this photo, Reisner (in white suit) carefully removes gold cylinder sheaths from the floor of the burial chamber while Dows Dunham (in shirt and tie), Tai Mohamed (in white galabiya and turban), and Ahmed M. (standing) look on. Lying on the ground at left are four vessels of Egyptian alabaster. [Mohammedani Ibrahim Ibrahim]

29 [overleaf]

Working in the tombs was both dangerous and uncomfortable. The floor was covered with accumulated water from summer rains, and dom palm logs were used to shore up the partly fallen roof. As Reisner reported, "Our architect, Mr. Robert Williams, experienced in more civilized ways of propping, was inclined to smile at our rough use of dom-logs; but Said Ahmed, the chief Egyptian foreman, vowed to sacrifice a sheep if we finished the work without accident; and whether because of this vow or because the place was not so dangerous as it looked, the excavation was finished in safety." Here, the architect records details of construction as he balances on a raft held steady by a Sudanese worker standing waist-deep in water. [Mohammedani Ibrahim Ibrahim]

30 [overleaf]

Two of the kings buried at Nuri, Anlamani and his brother and successor Aspelta, had enormous sarcophagi made of granite gneiss from the Tombos quarry near the Third Cataract. Anlamani's burial chamber lies more than twelve feet underground. The sarcophagus and its lid had to be dragged through two outer chambers and up a stairway of fifty-seven steep steps to reach the surface. On this day, the lid has made it halfway up the stairs. Note the light-rail tracks laid to help with the process. [Mohammedani Ibrahim Ibrahim]

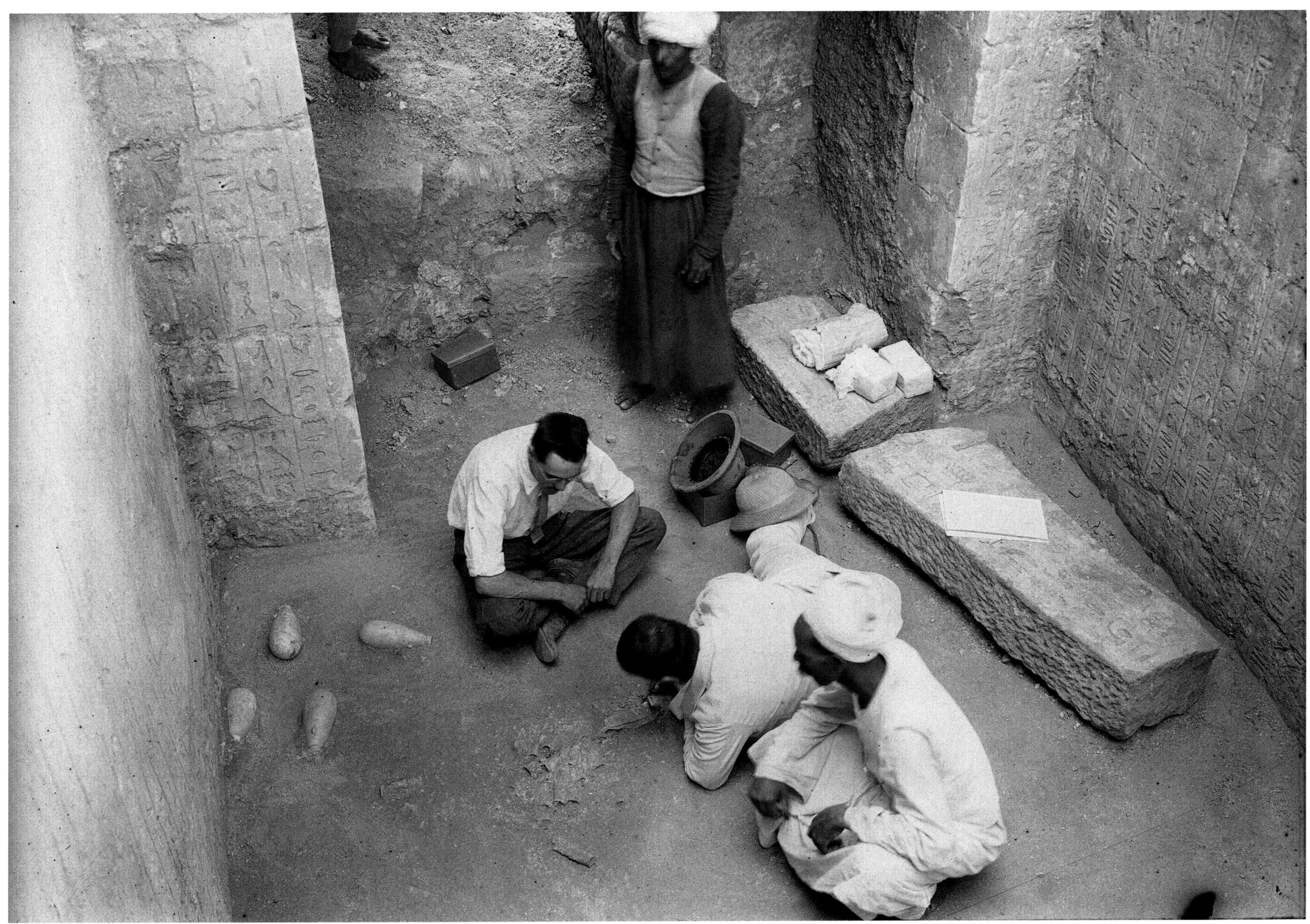

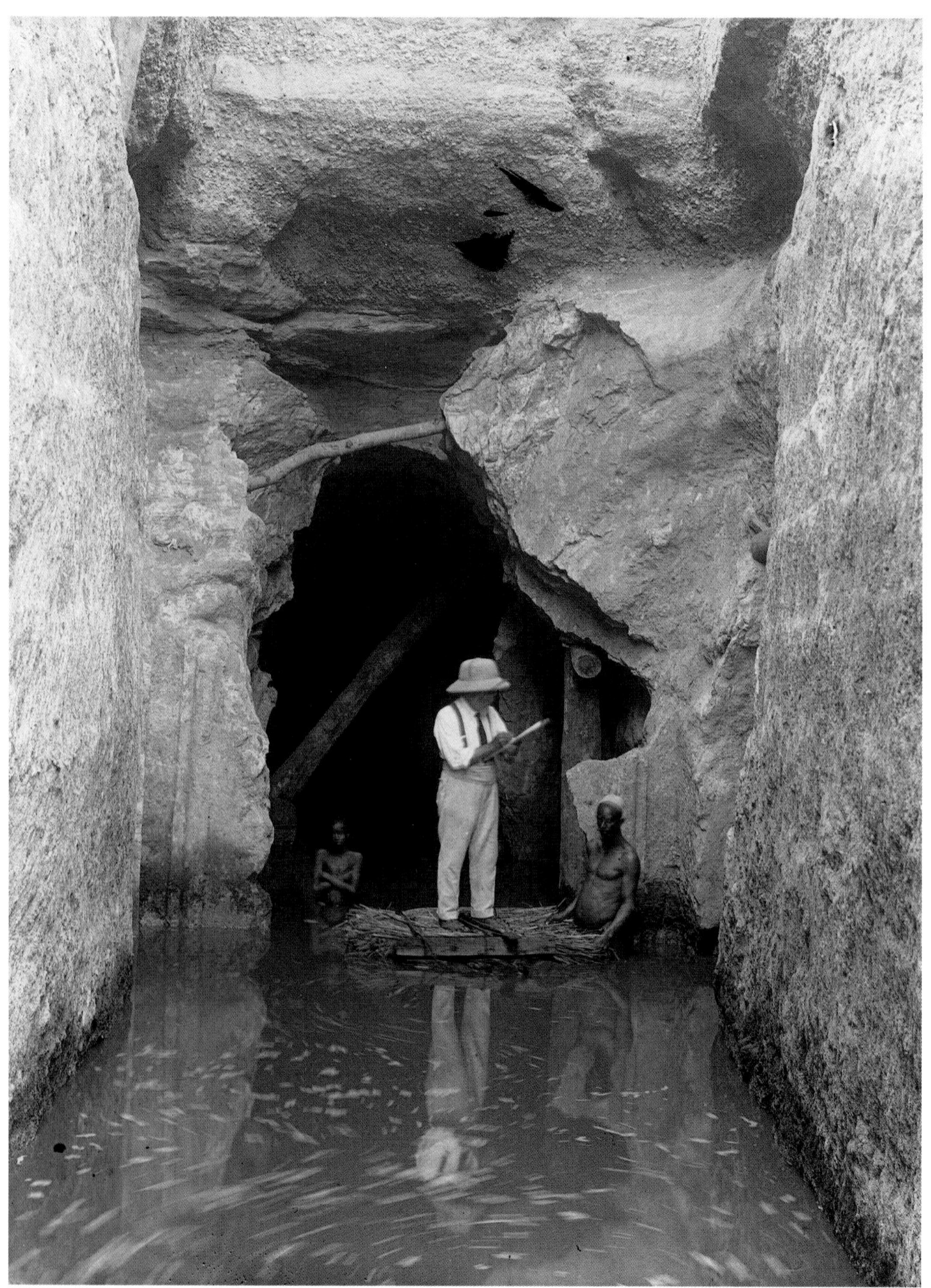

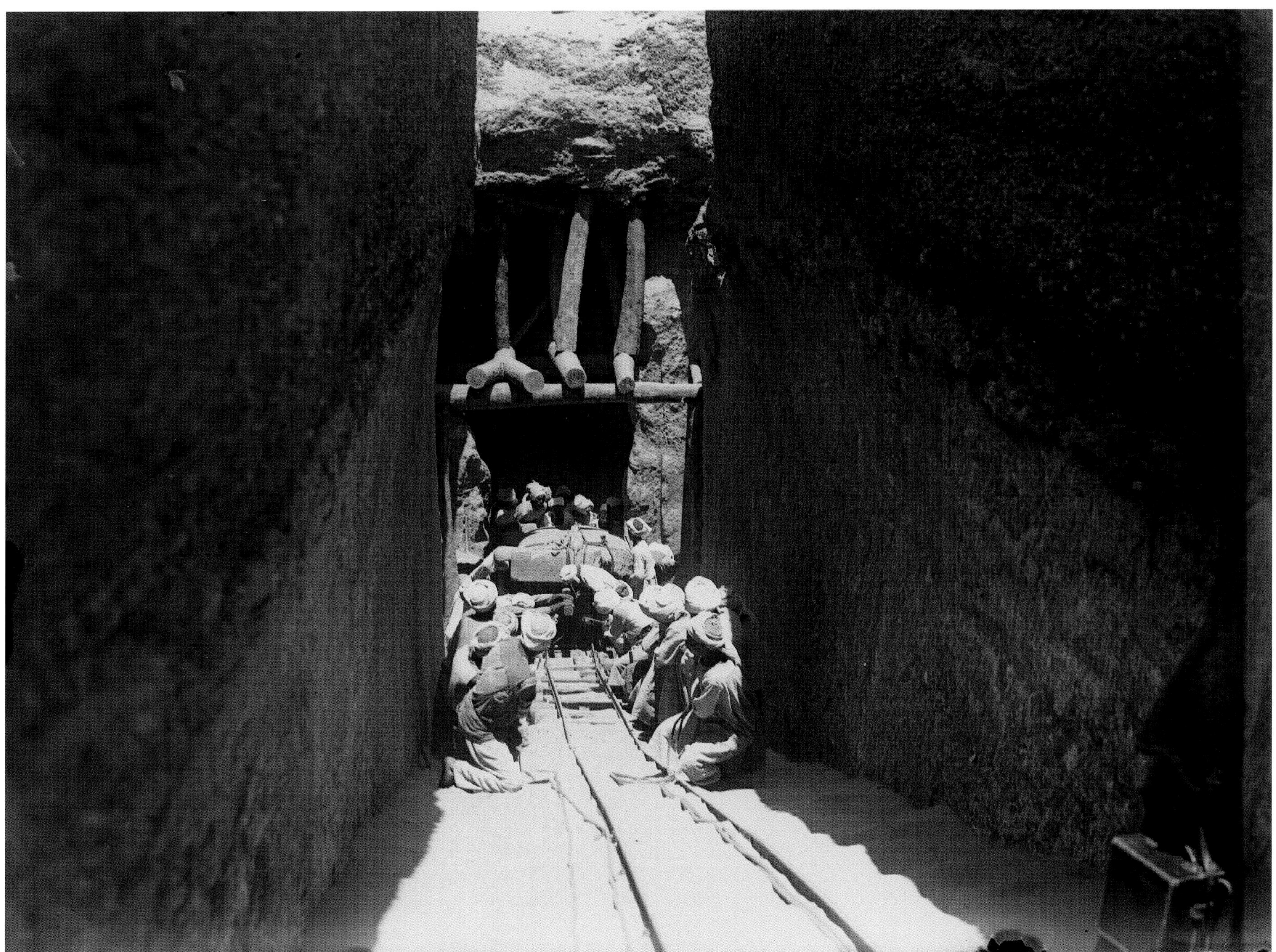

31
Six days later, the massive stone box is lifted out of the tomb. The king's pyramid is in the
background. [Mohammedani Ibrahim Ibrahim]

32–33 [overleaf]
Raised up from the tomb where they had lain for thirteen hundred years, the box and its lid
sit on rails incongruously amid houses and palm trees. Anlamani's sarcophagus is now in
the Sudan National Museum in Khartoum. The even larger sarcophagus of his brother Aspelta
is in Boston. [Mohammedani Ibrahim Ibrahim]

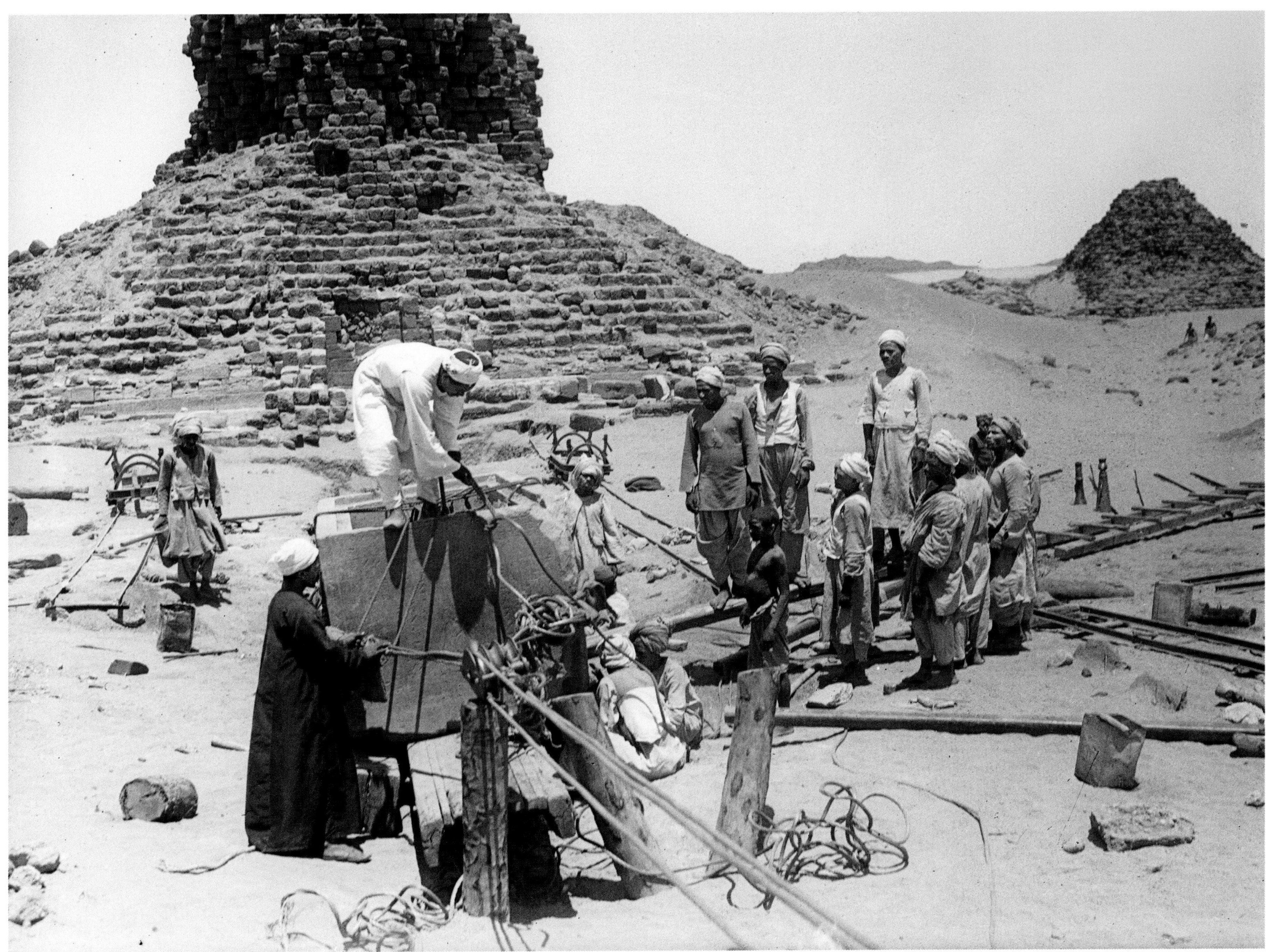

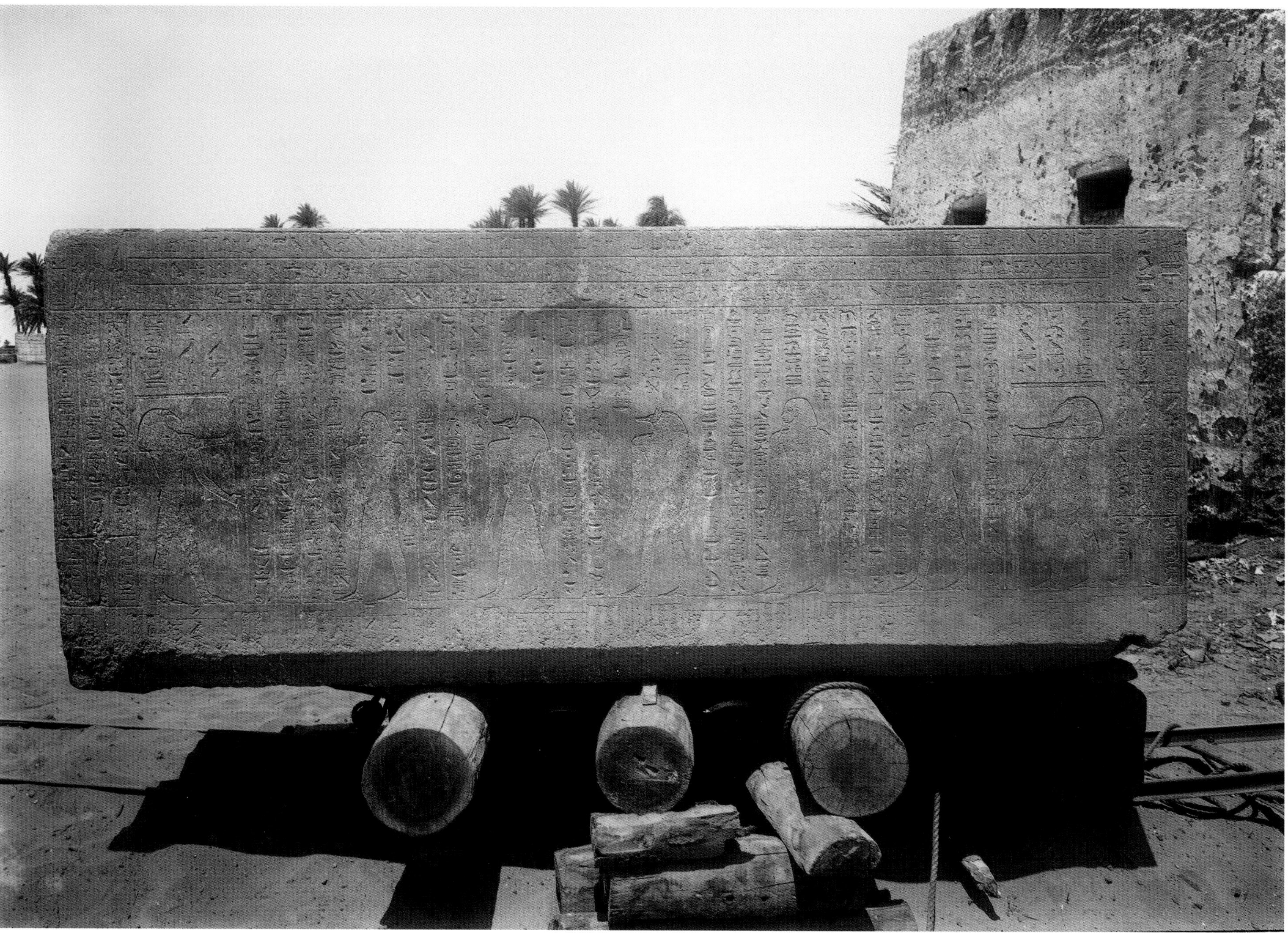

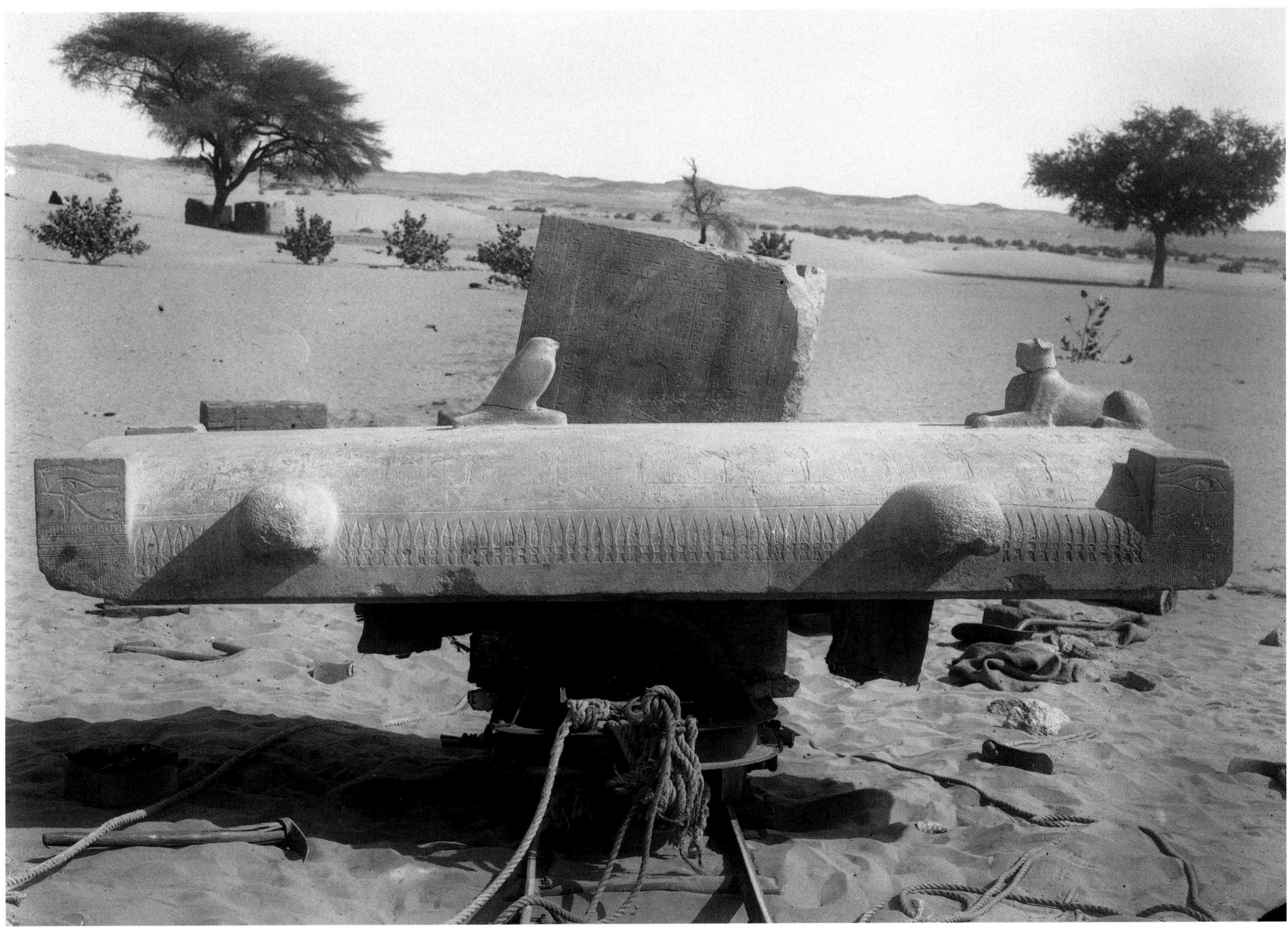

34

A solitary sandstone butte dominates the landscape on the west bank of the Nile. This is Gebel
Barkal, or Mount Barkal, known in ancient times as the Holy Mountain and believed to be
the dwelling place of the god Amen of Napata. Temples clustered on its eastern side. Seen
from afar and reduced to their foundations, they seem to merge into the mountainside.
[Mohammedani Ibrahim Ibrahim]

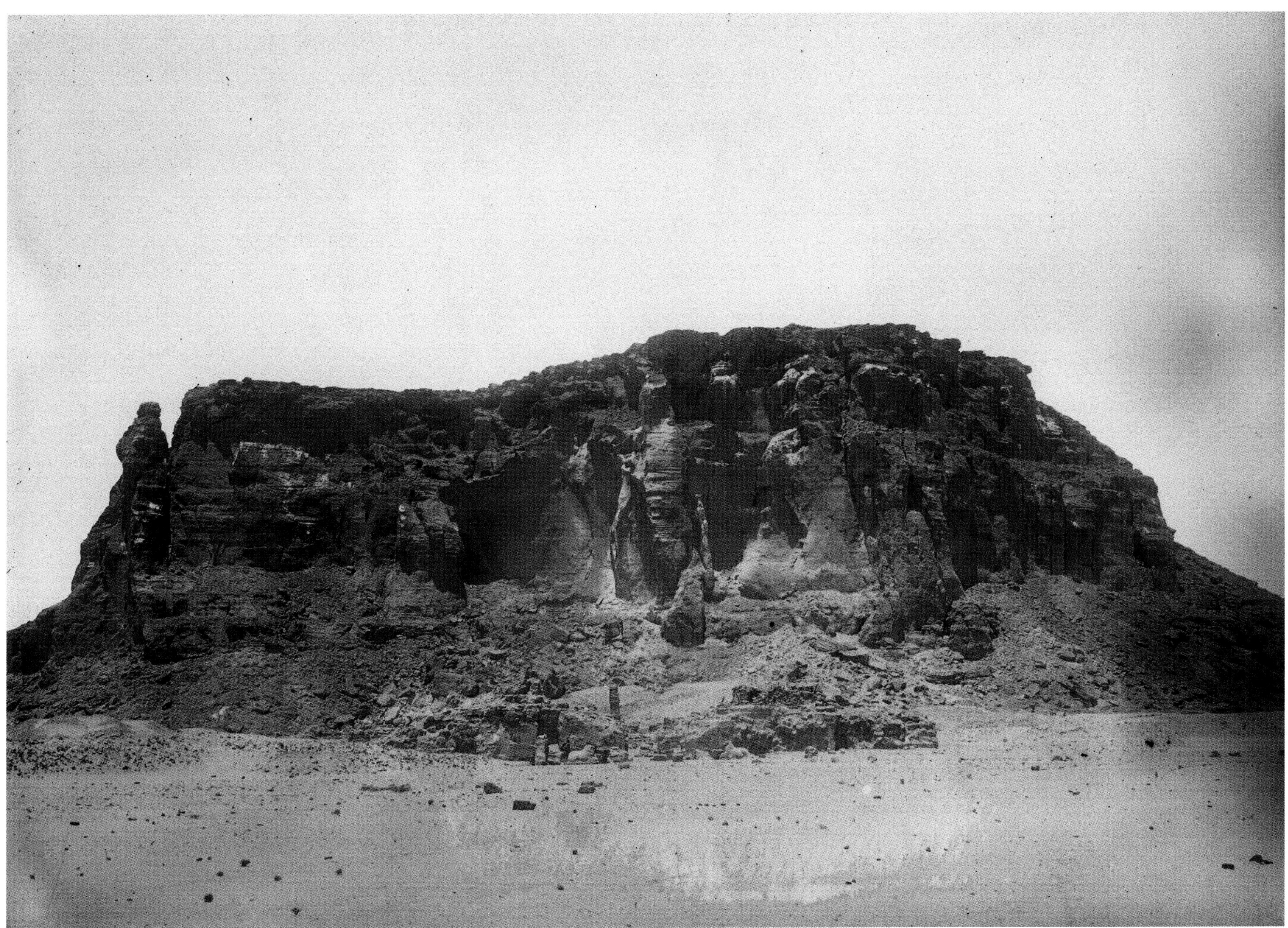

35

Looking down from the mountaintop, the ground plan of the Great Temple of Amen of Napata, partially cleared of debris, unfolds before us. Its full extent is 535 feet (160 meters) from the rear of the sanctuary to the entrance gateway, making it the largest temple ever built in Sudan. [Mahmud Shadduf]

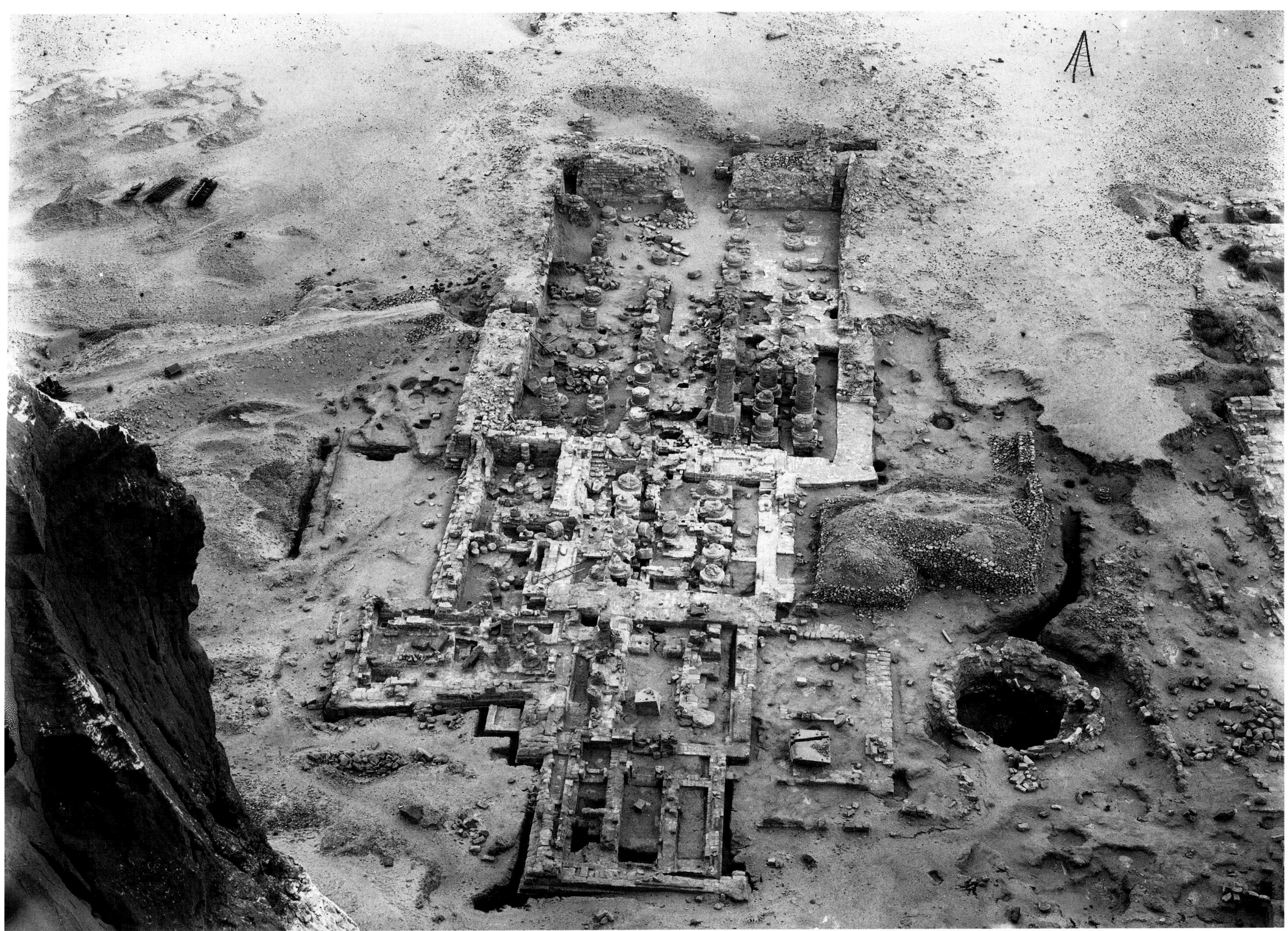

36

South of the Great Temple of Amen is a temple dedicated to Amen's consort, the goddess Mut. Its most conspicuous remains are two columns with capitals in the form of the head of the goddess Hathor, a woman with cow's ears. The two columns incline slightly toward each other, as though the goddesses were whispering shared secrets. [Mahmud Shadduf]

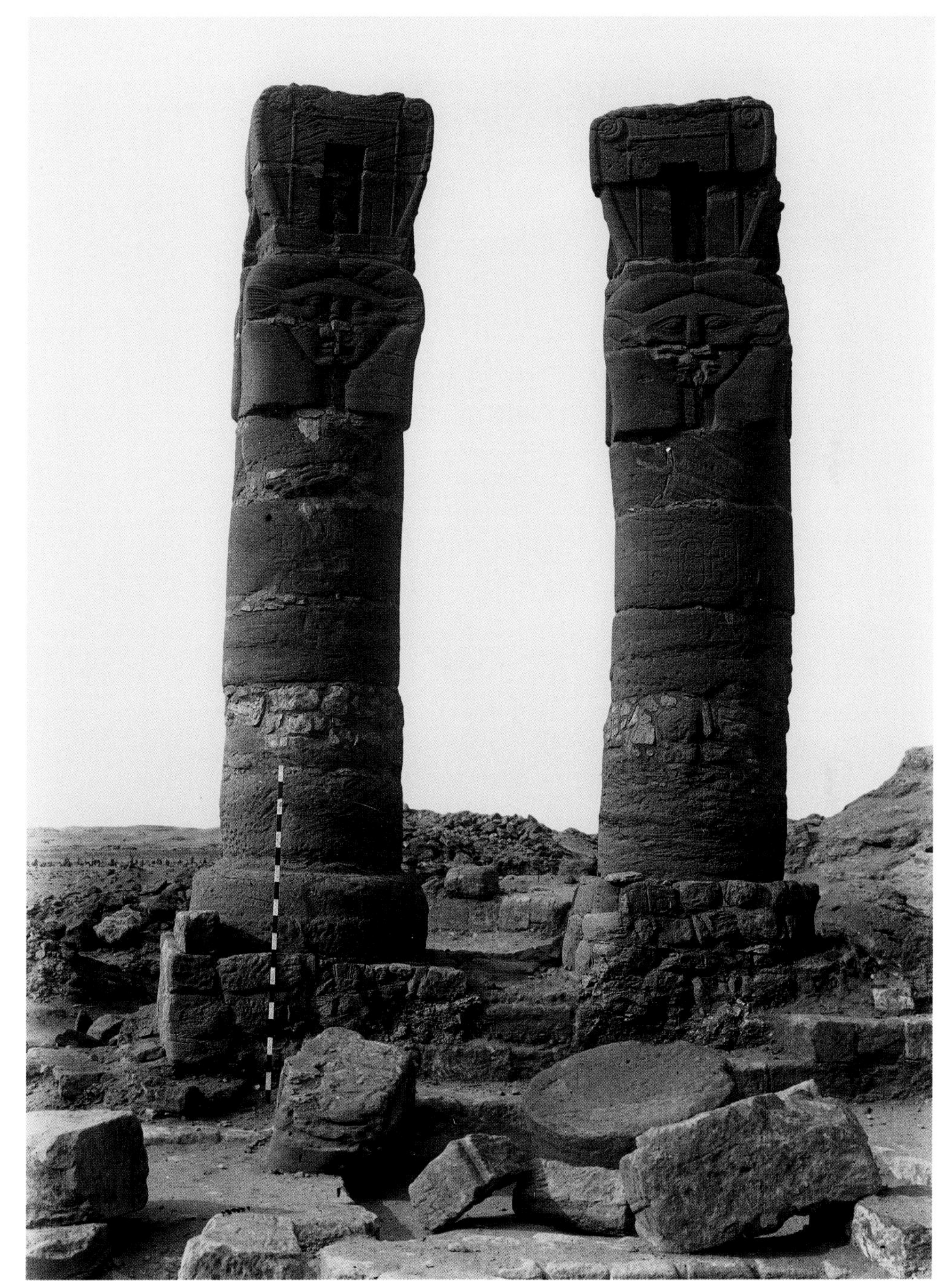

37
A visit to the pyramid of Senkamanisken at Nuri. Reisner is in the center. Behind him, with their mounts, are his daughter Mary Reisner, Mrs. Reisner, and Mrs. Symons, secretary. The Sudanese are hard at work in the right foreground. In the background is the Decauville light rail used to transport debris. There is an implicit social hierarchy in this casual scene, with the expedition staff on one side, in their white suits and riding outfits, and the local workers on the other. [Mohammedani Ibrahim Ibrahim]

38 [overleaf]
Reisner gives William Jackson Pasha, the governor of Dongola Province, and his party a tour of the newly cleared sanctuary of the temple of Atlanersa at Gebel Barkal. The headless statue in the foreground is now in the MFA.

39 [overleaf]
This photo shows the different floor levels corresponding to different phases of construction of the temple. The addition of a table and chair creates an improvised work station. [Mahmud Shadduf]

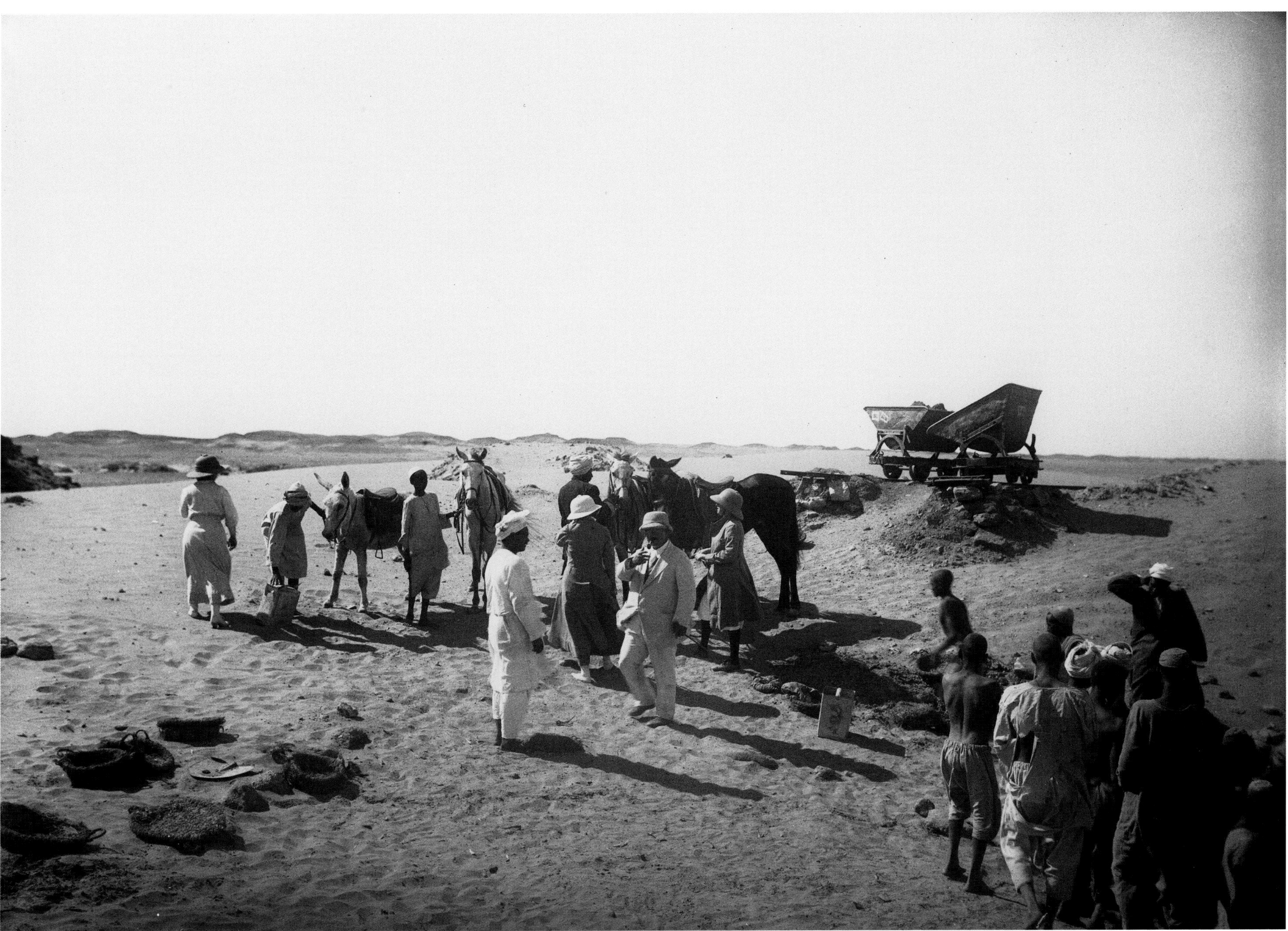

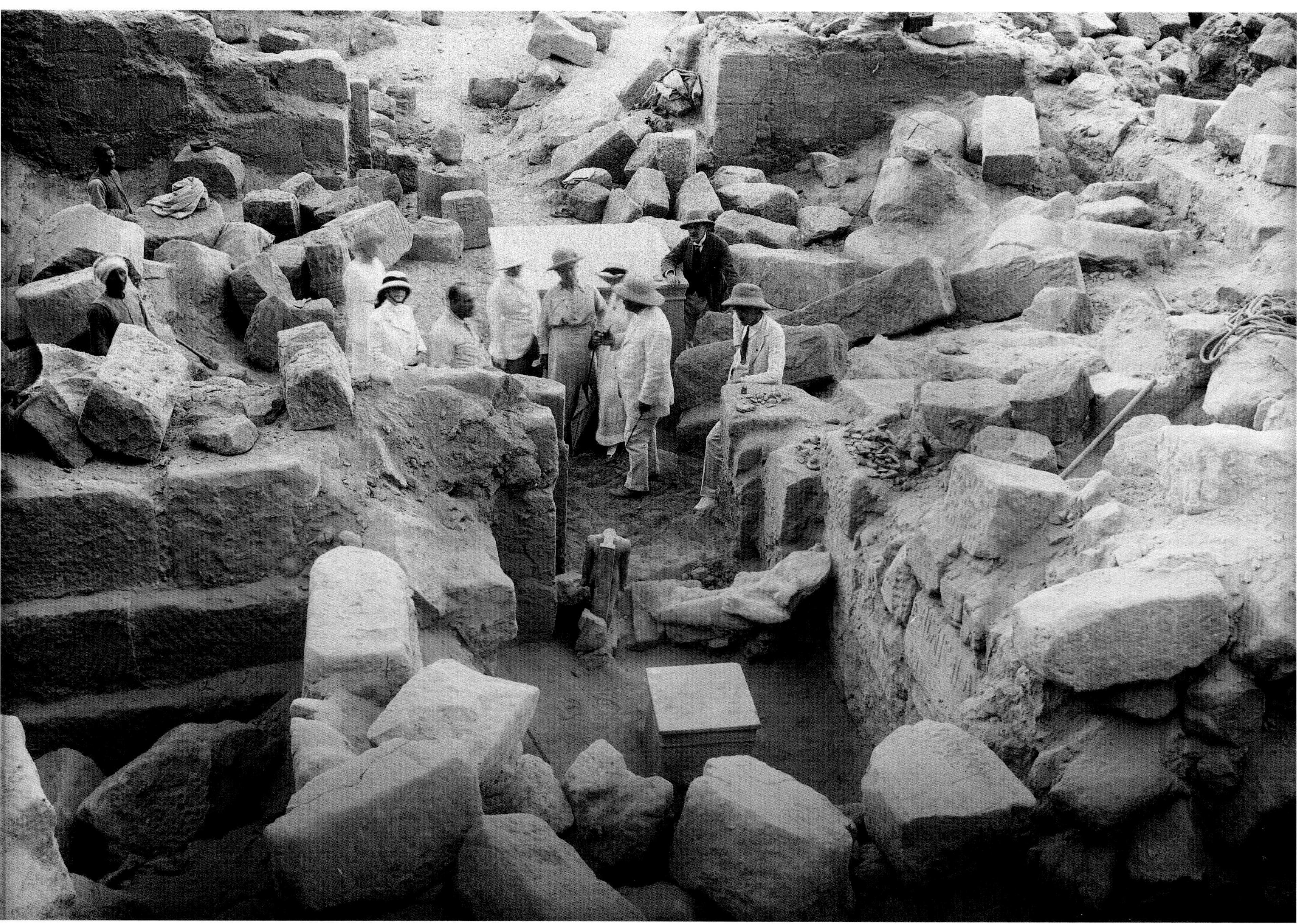

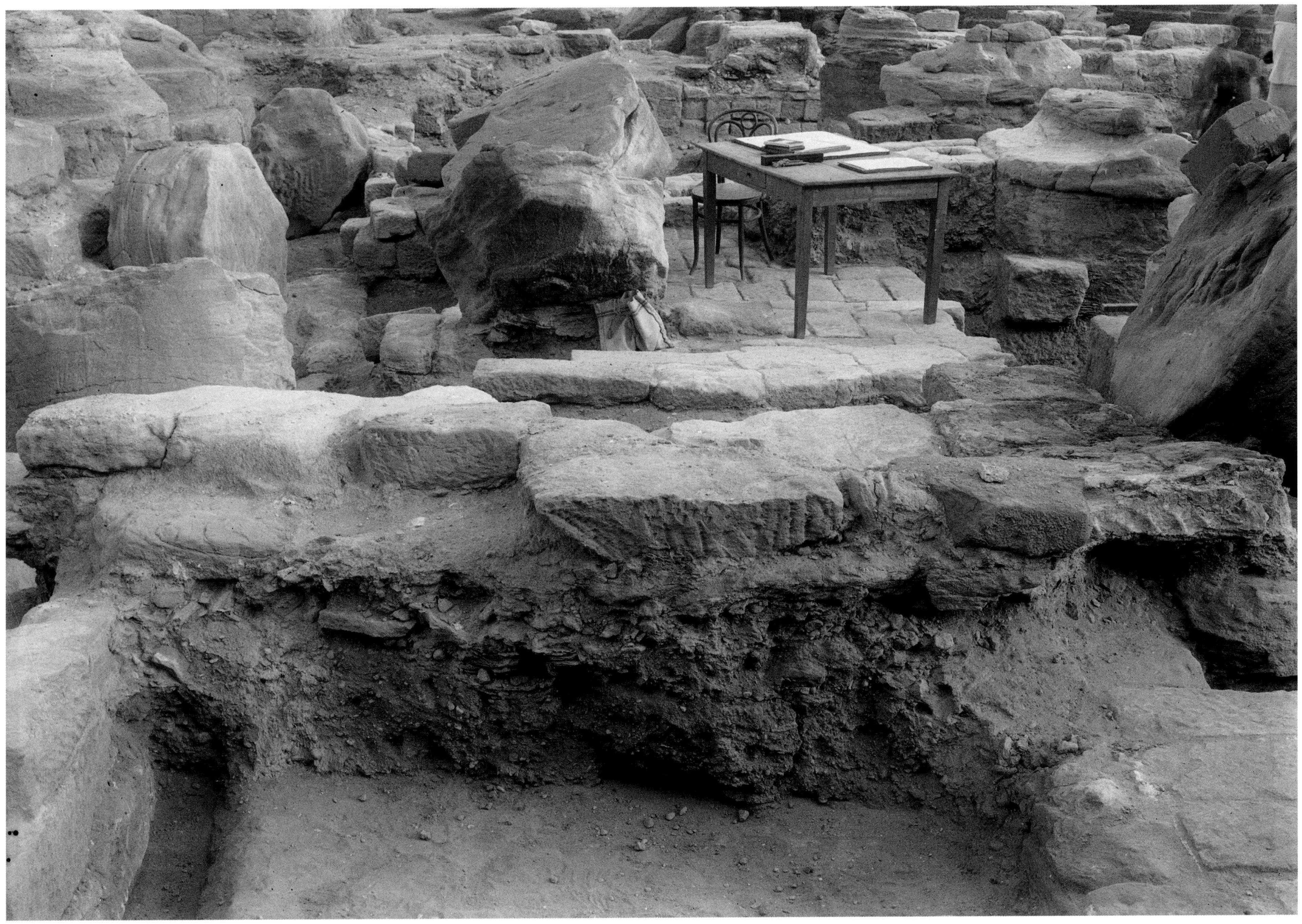

40

The director at work. Here, at Gebel Barkal, Reisner uses a theodolite, a surveyor's instrument
for measuring horizontal and vertical angles to obtain precise dimensions for mapping.
[Mohammedani Ibrahim Ibrahim]

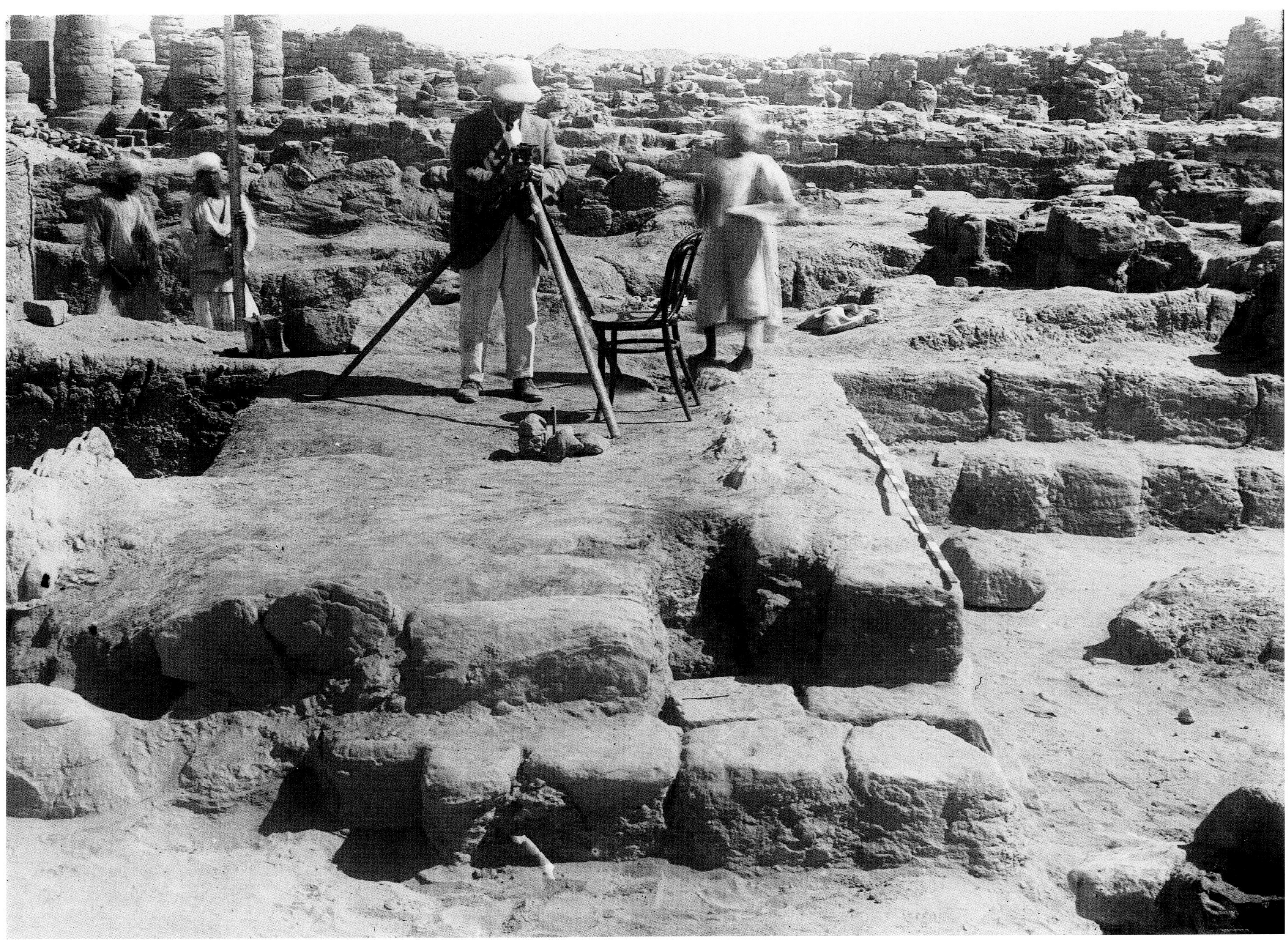

41
Workers carrying baskets full of debris up out of a pyramid at Nuri to the dumping ground.
[Mohammedani Ibrahim Ibrahim]

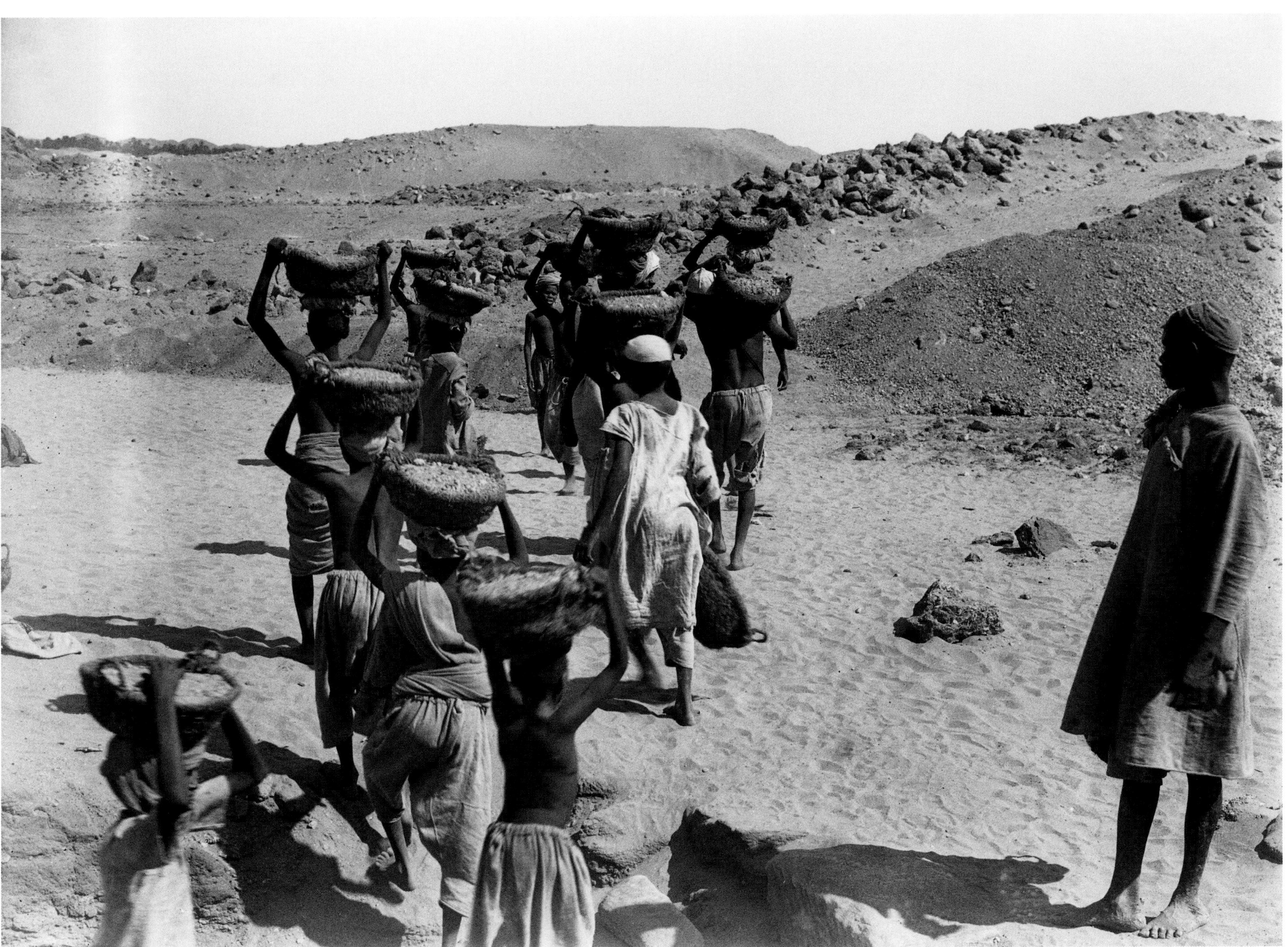

42

Payday at Gebel Barkal: The workers line up in front of the tent to receive their wages. In front of
the tent is an *angareb*, a traditional Sudanese bed made of wood covered with a network of
rope or rawhide. [Mohammedani Ibrahim Ibrahim]

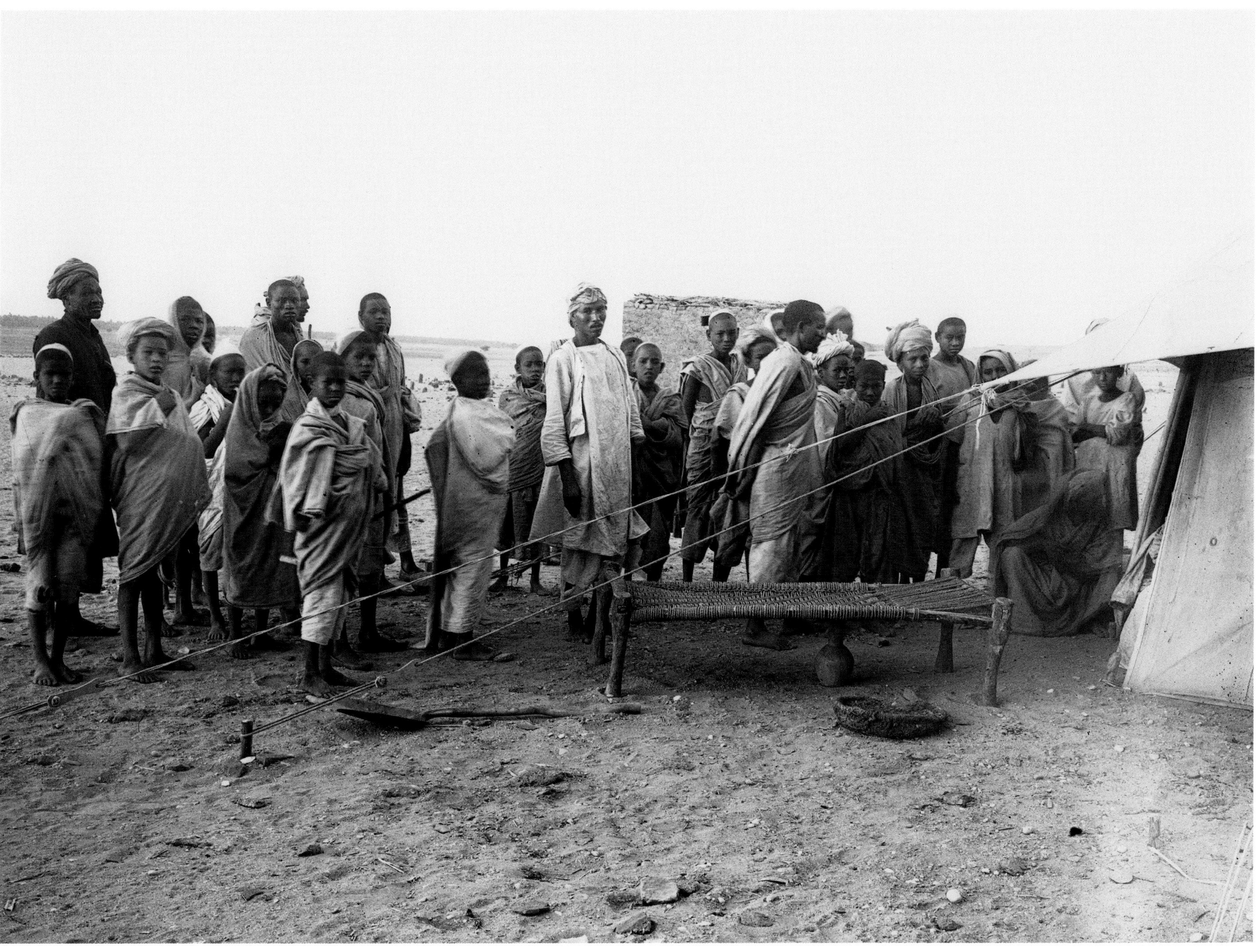

43–46
The Egyptian photographers, who like the Europeans and Americans were strangers in northern
Sudan, documented the local people and customs. [Mohammedani Ibrahim Ibrahim]

47 [overleaf]
Photographers laid out smaller finds in clever patterns, employing a fine sense of design.
Shown here are strings of beads of faience and semiprecious stones found in the graves at Kerma.
The centerpiece is a glazed quartz crystal pendant left "in the rough." [Mahmud Shadduf]

48 [overleaf]
These faience and gold amulets were found in tombs at the West Cemetery at Meroe (Begrawiya).
[Bedawi Ahmed Abu Bukr]

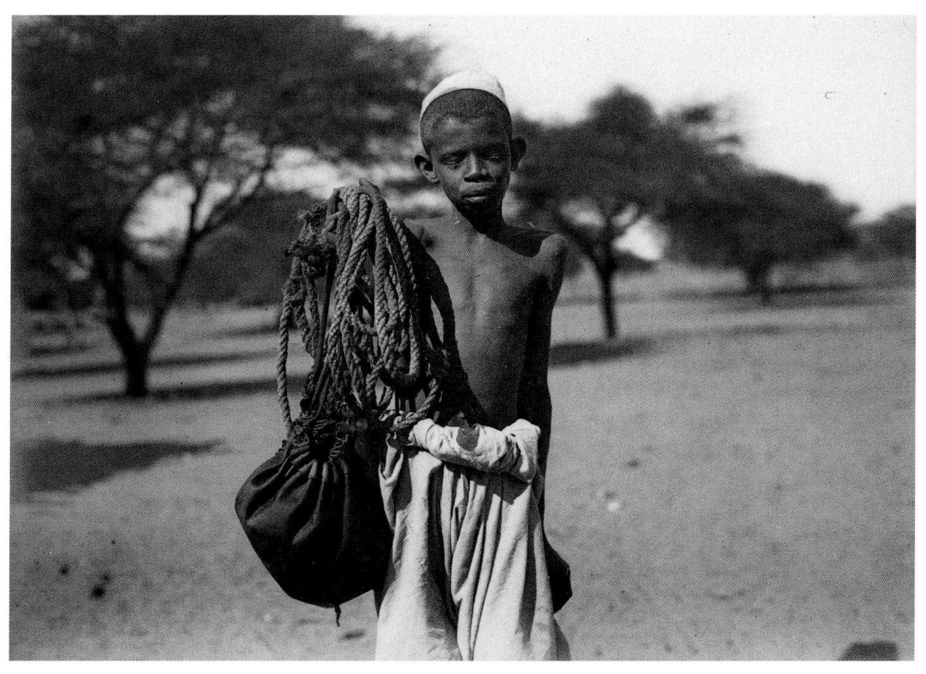
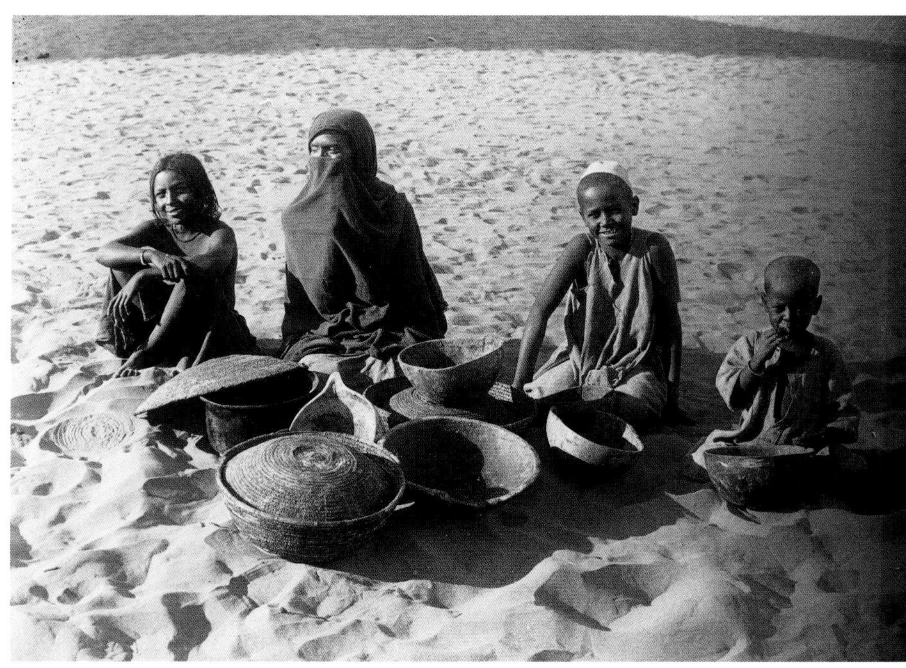
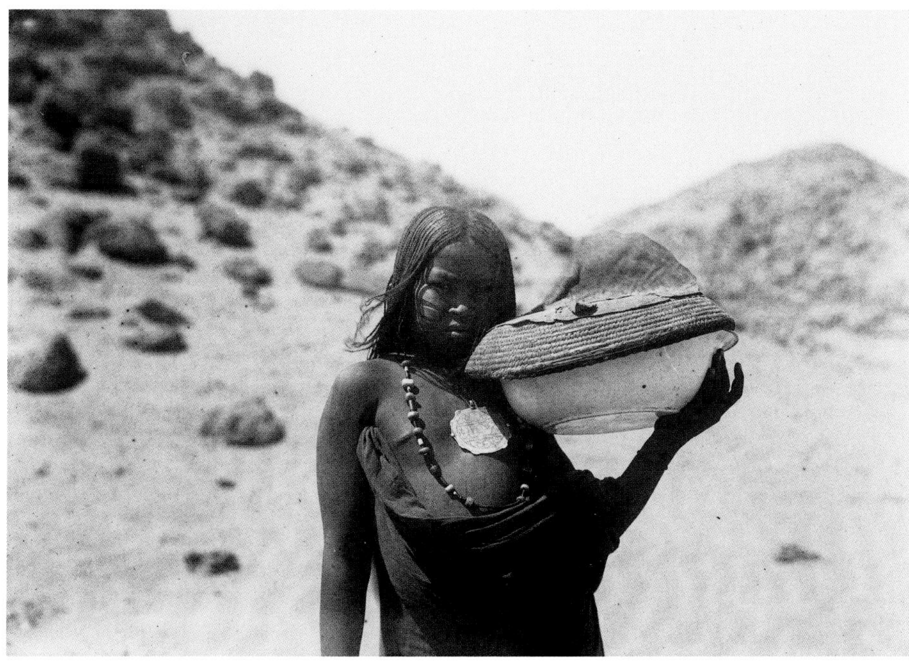
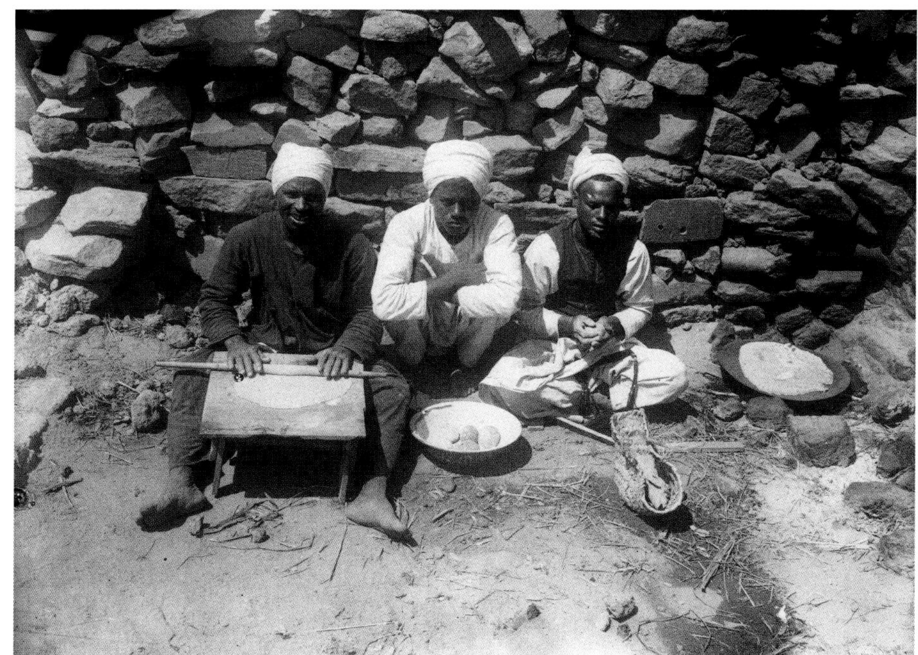

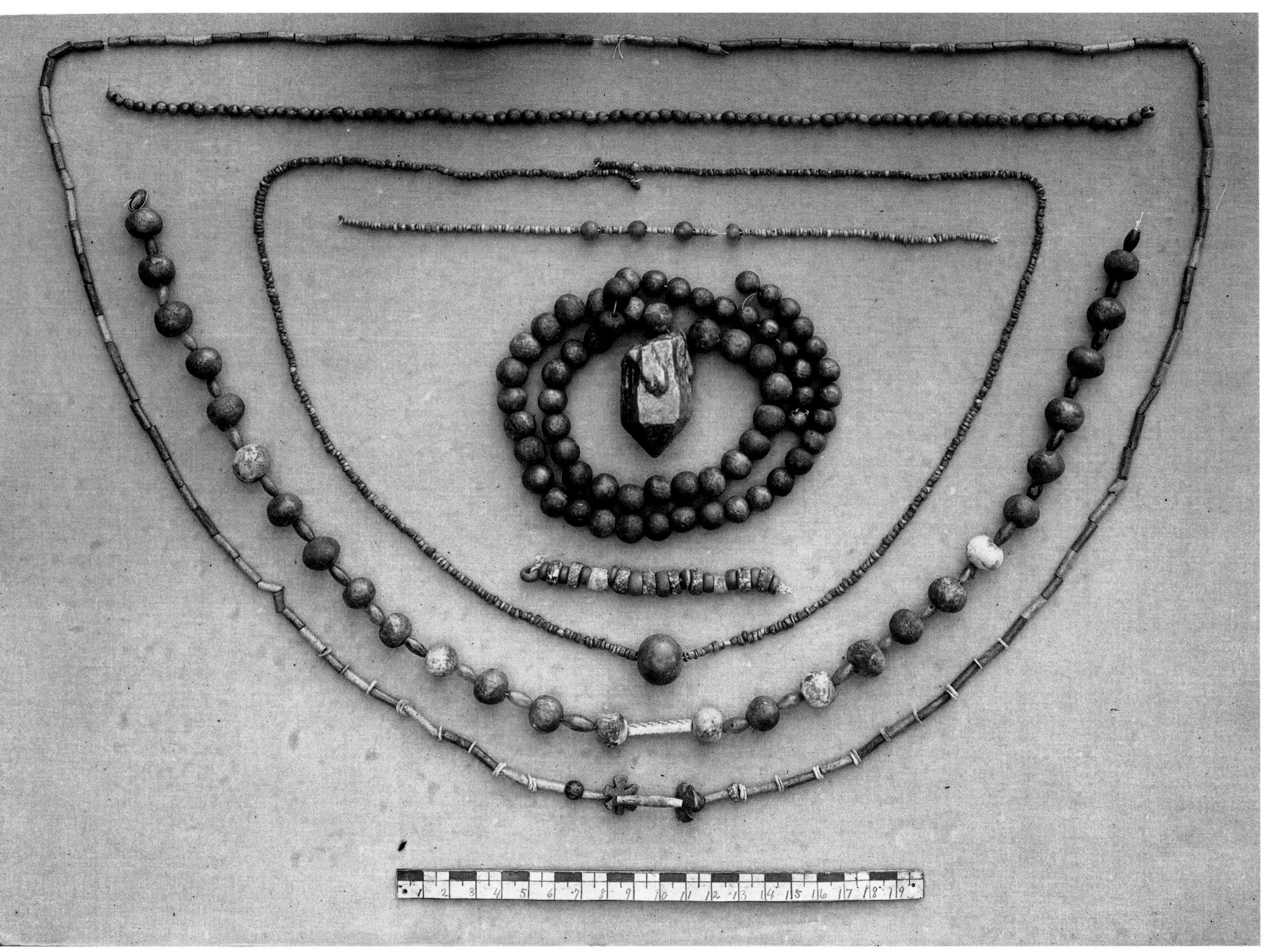

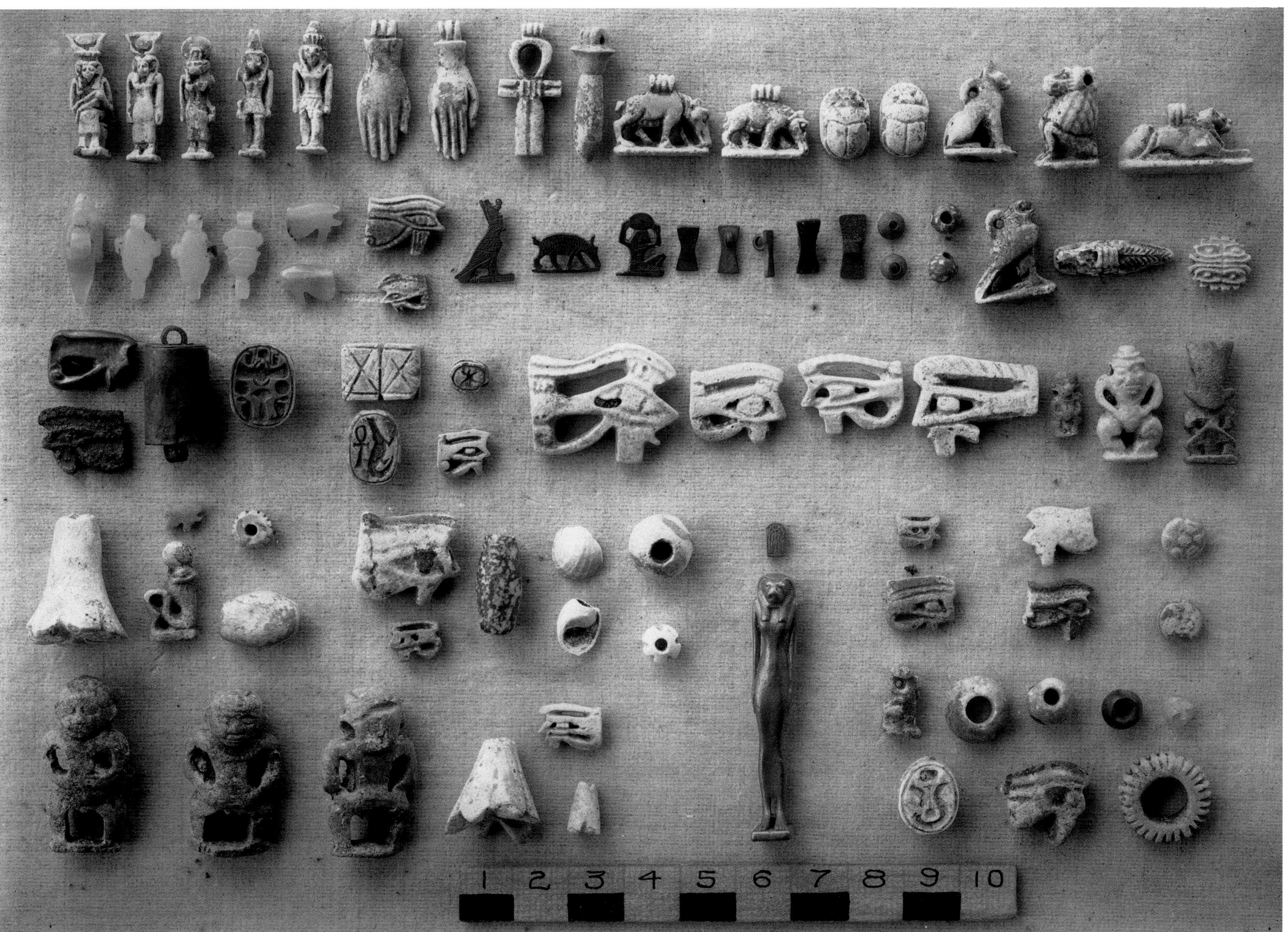

1 2 3 4 5 6 7 8 9 10

49

Ostrich-feather fans were a standard component of the burial equipment in the elite graves at Kerma. Despite its delicate appearance, this fan survived for some thirty-five hundred years. [Mahmud Shadduf]

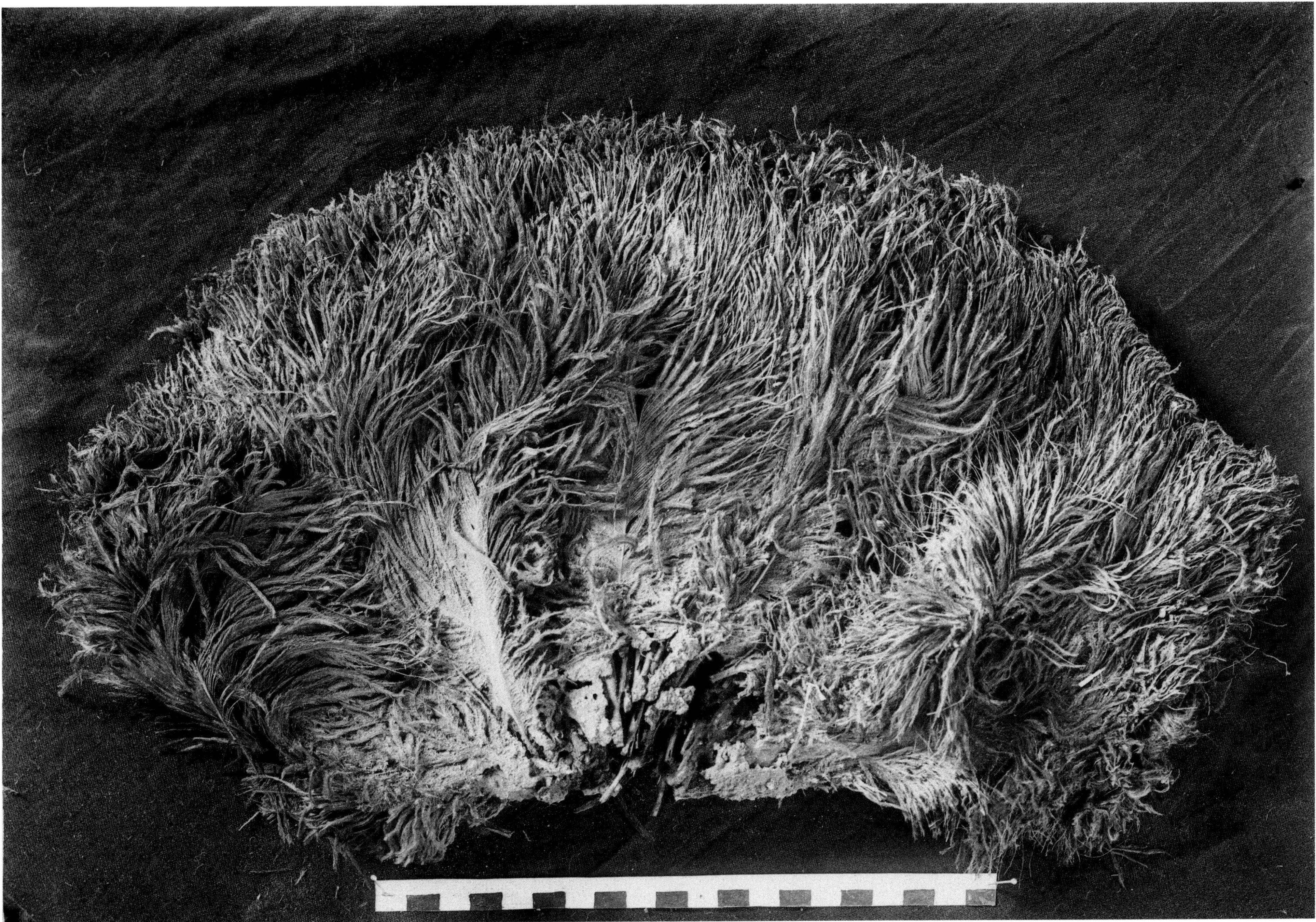

50

These ivory inlays once decorated the footboards of wooden beds. They take the form of geometric shapes, animals, and animal-headed deities such as the hippopotamus-headed goddess Taweret. The animals include both real species (rhinoceros, lion, and vulture) and mythical beasts (winged cobra and giraffe). The arrangement in the photo does not reproduce the way they would have appeared on the beds. [Mohammedani Ibrahim Ibrahim]

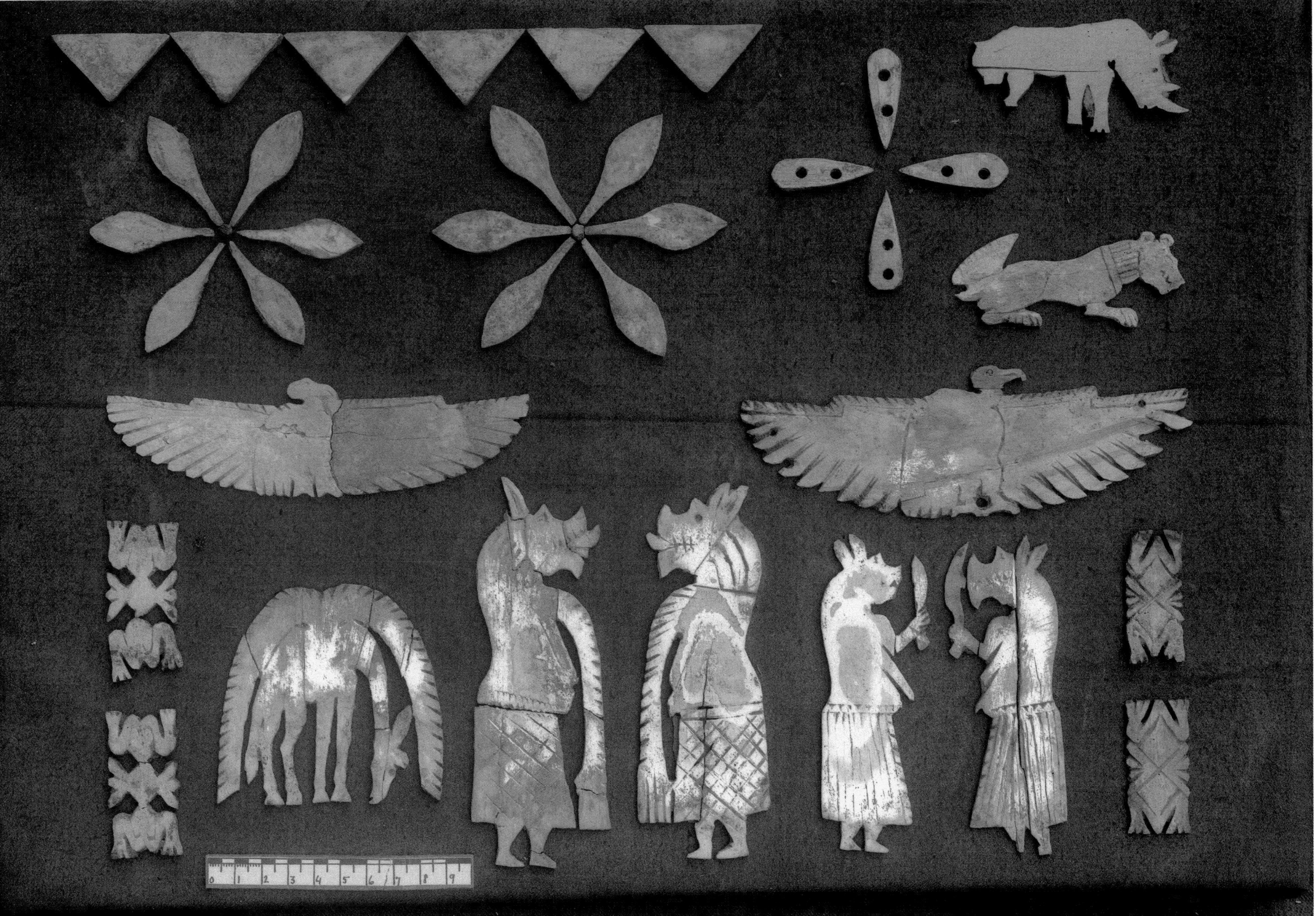

51

Thin copper-sheet lion inlays from Kerma once adorned the footboard of a wooden bed, where they were arranged in four rows of four, just as they appear in the photo. The upper two lions were on the inside of the footboard. [Mahmud Shadduf]

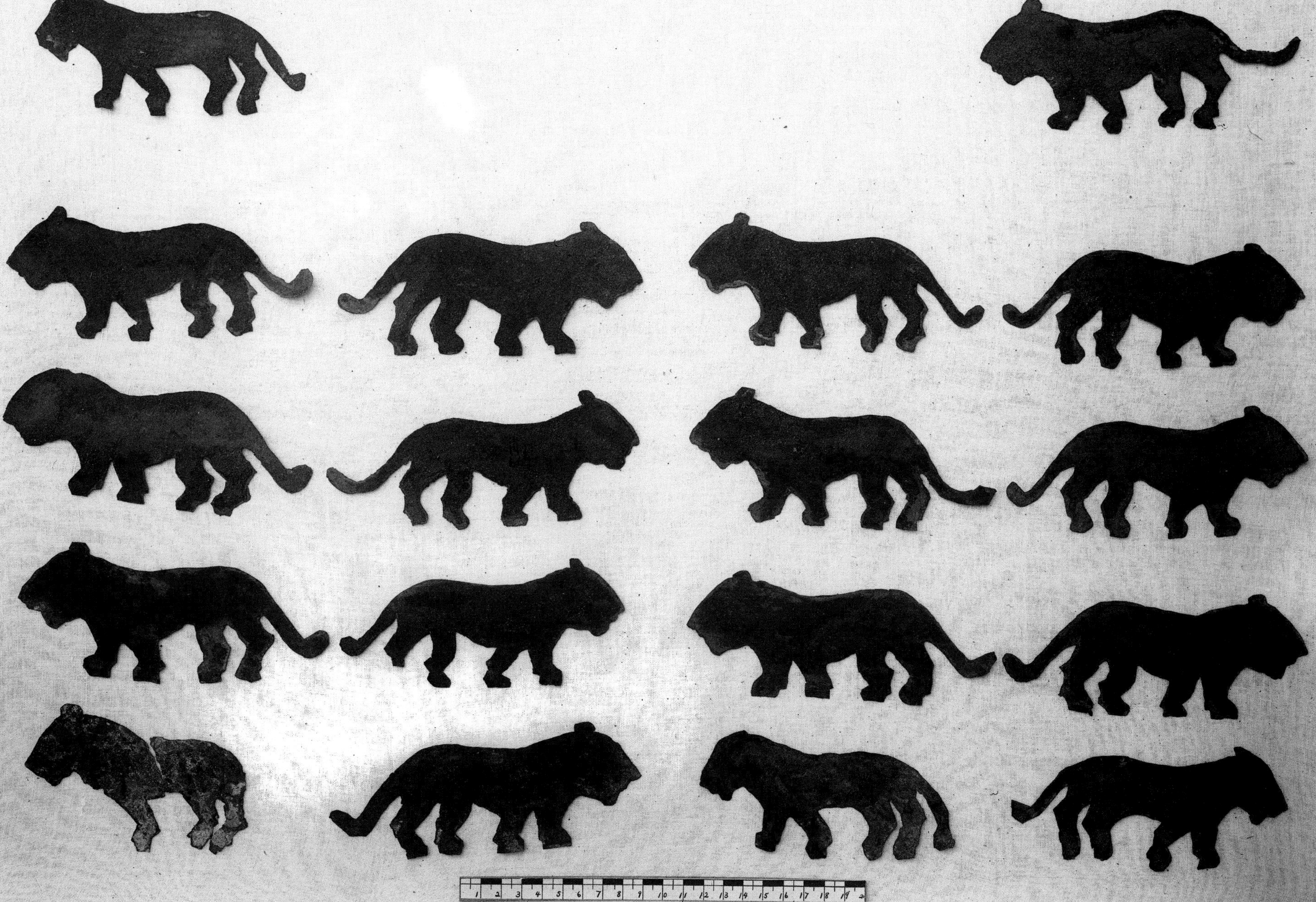

52

An assortment of objects from Kerma includes a wooden dish or spoon, stone palettes for grinding eye paint, a bronze angle brace for a stool or bed, two bronze knife blades, and two bronze daggers with wood and ivory handles. The hatchet-shaped objects are razors. The flies are military decorations. [Mahmud Shadduf]

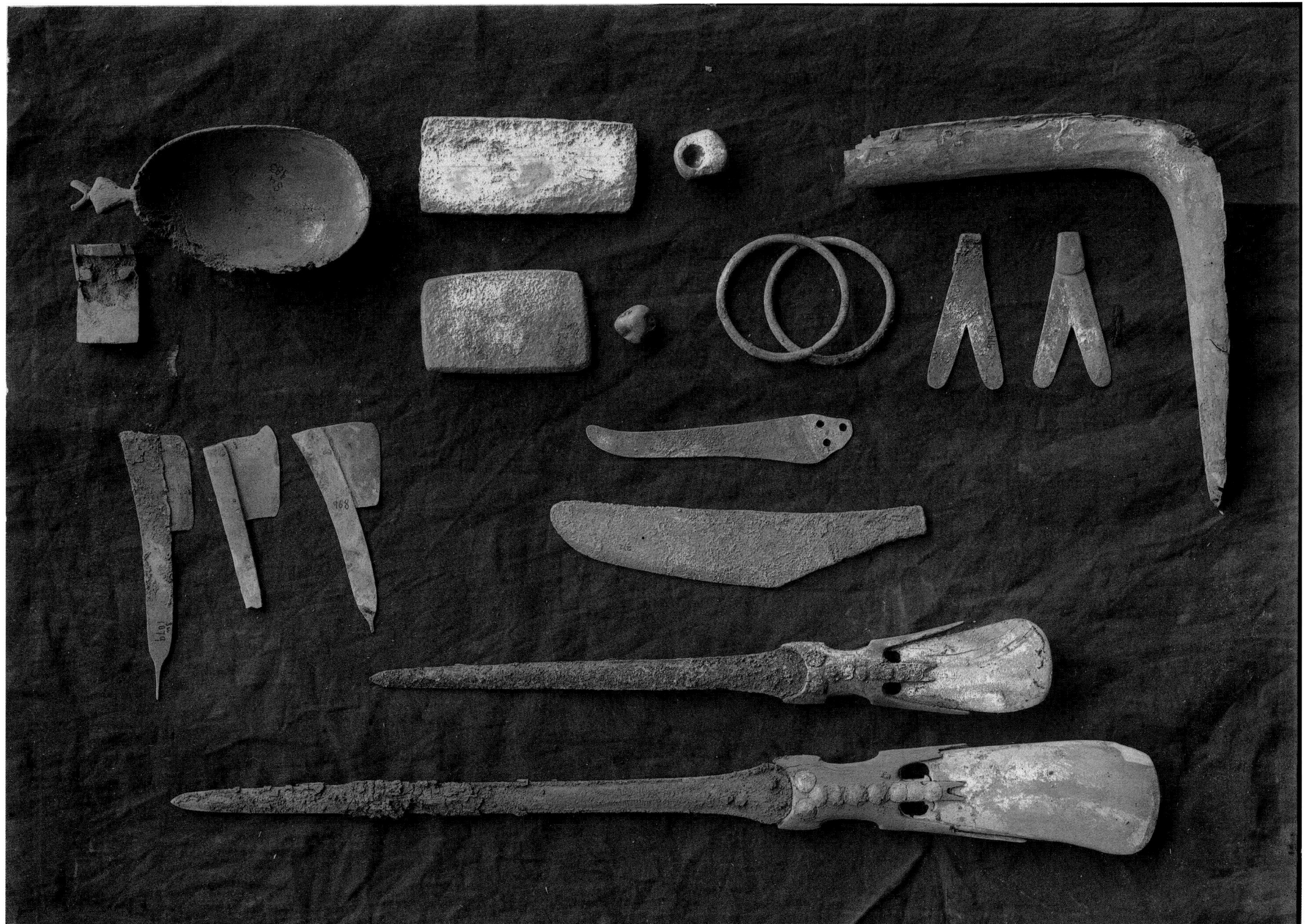

53

A mass of strung green glazed crystal beads from Kerma. [Mahmud Shadduf]

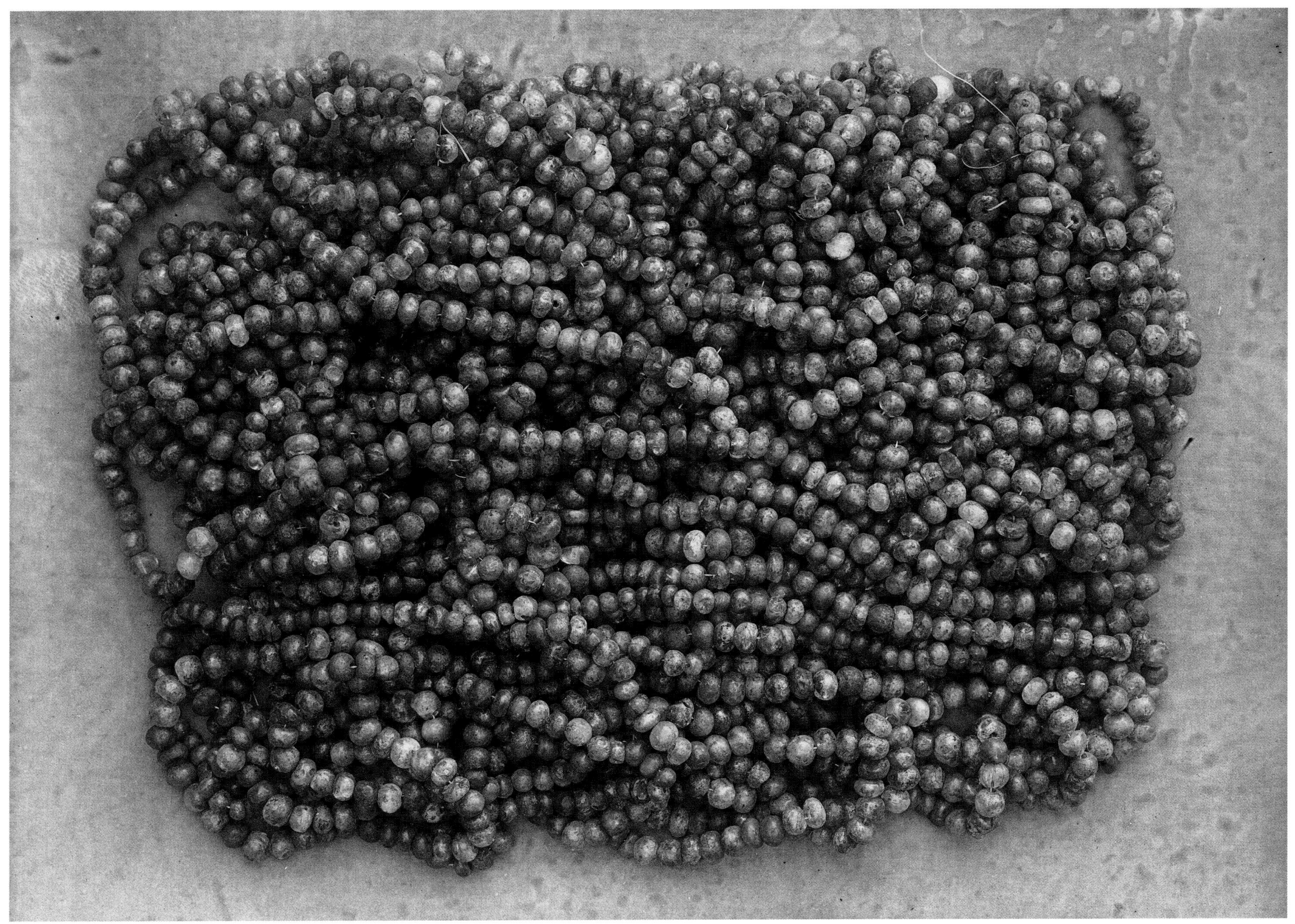

54

The royal mummies at Nuri were encased in nested sets of wooden coffins. These three pairs of inlay eyes (with eyelids of bronze, eyeballs of Egyptian alabaster, and pupils of obsidian) are all that remain of the three coffins of Queen Malakaye (r. 664–653 BC). The eyes on the bottom row have been placed upside down. [Mohammedani Ibrahim Ibrahim]

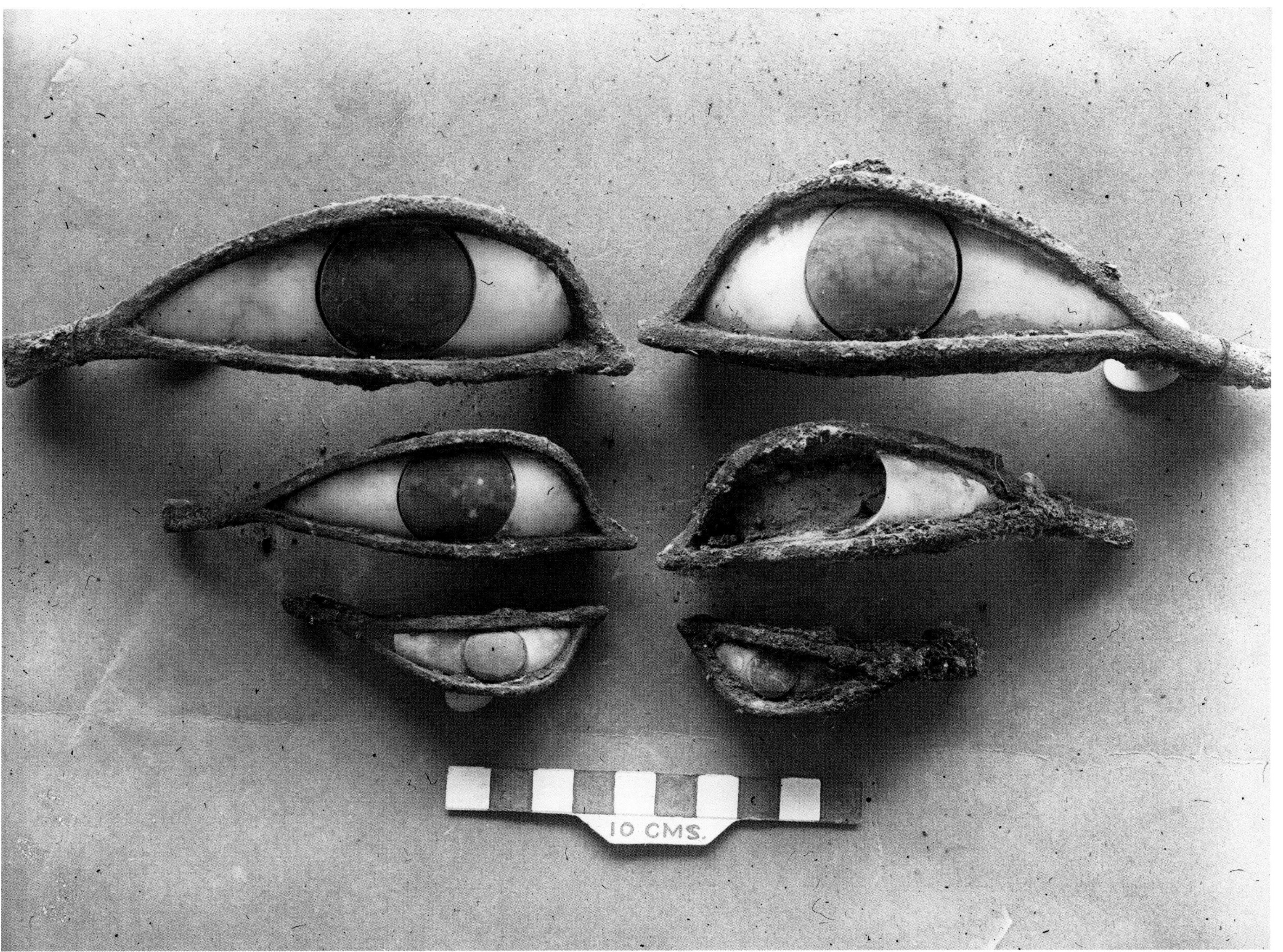
10 CMS.

55

The amount of Greek and Roman material found at Meroe attests to important trade contacts
between Nubia and the Mediterranean. The right hand and sandaled left foot belonged to
a Hellenistic Period bronze statuette of Dionysos. The bent left arm and lower left leg are smaller
and come from a different statuette. [Mohammedani Ibrahim Ibrahim]

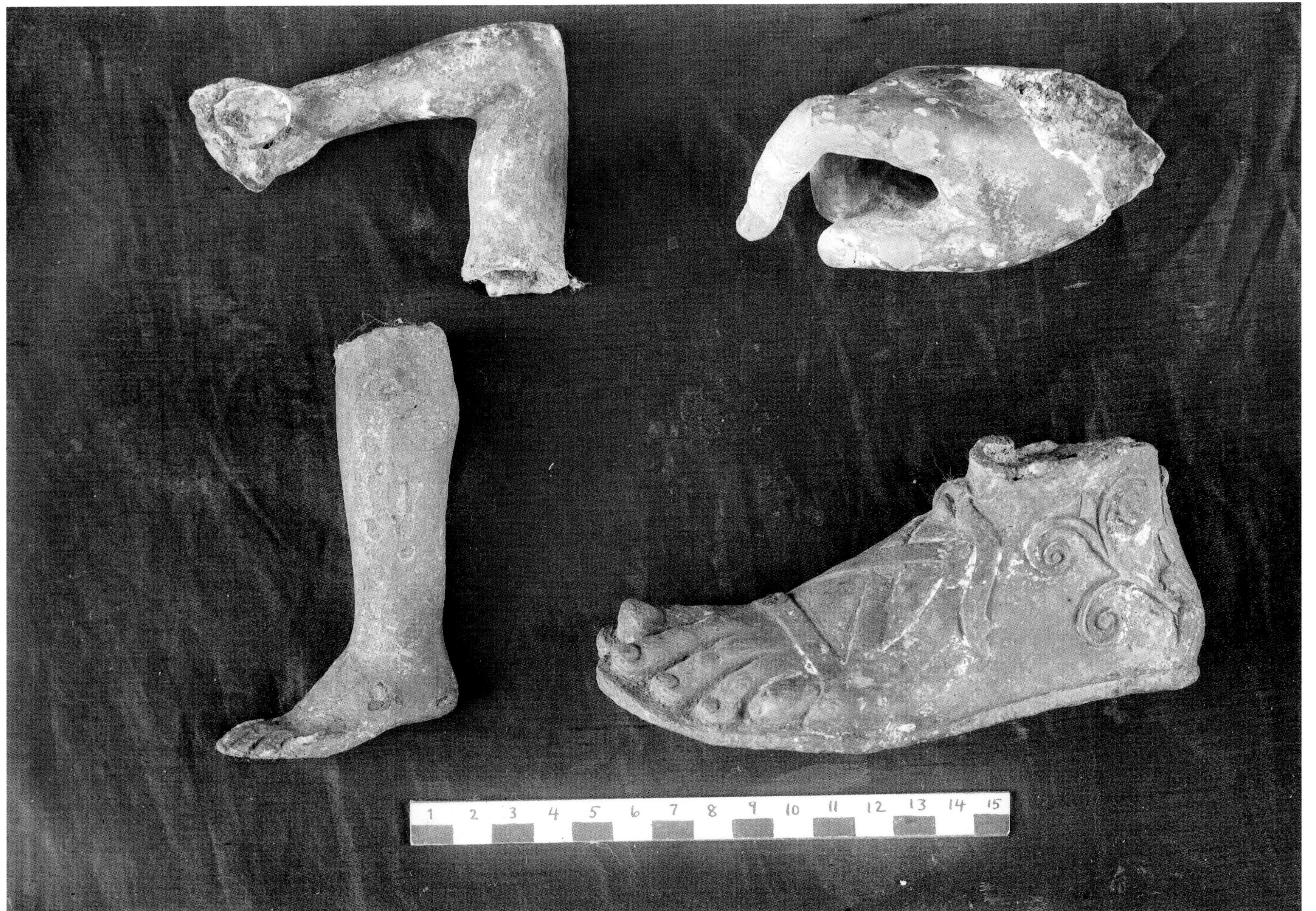

56

A number of Roman bronze lamps with figural handles were found in the tombs at Meroe. This one,
in the form of a galloping centaur, would have cast striking shadows on the wall at banquets.
[Mohammedani Ibrahim Ibrahim]

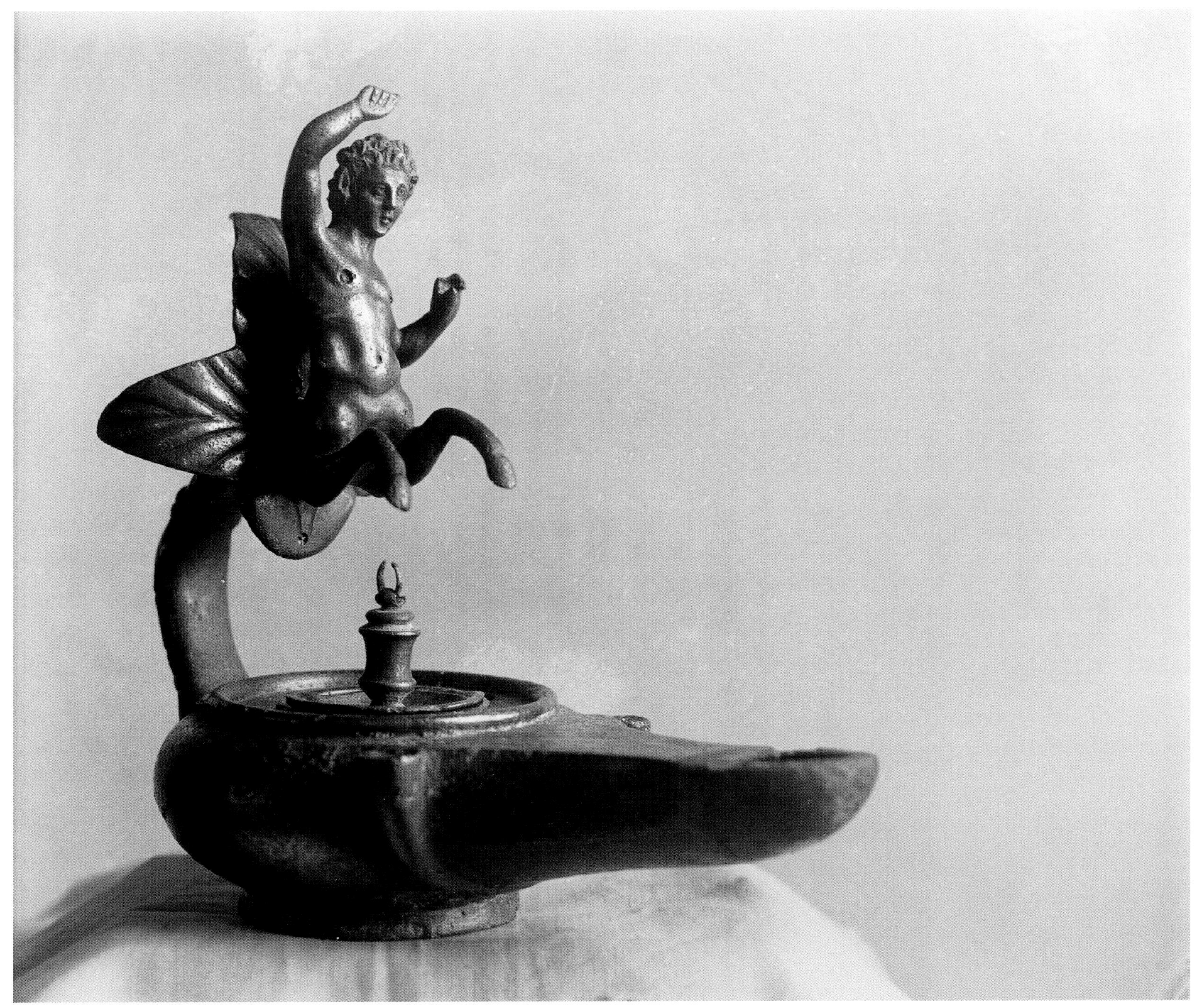

57

The interior walls of the funerary chapels were decorated in relief with offering scenes. Here, an unnamed queen sits on a lion throne in a kiosk. Before her, a male attendant offers incense, while behind her the goddess Isis spreads protective wings. [Mohammedani Ibrahim Ibrahim]

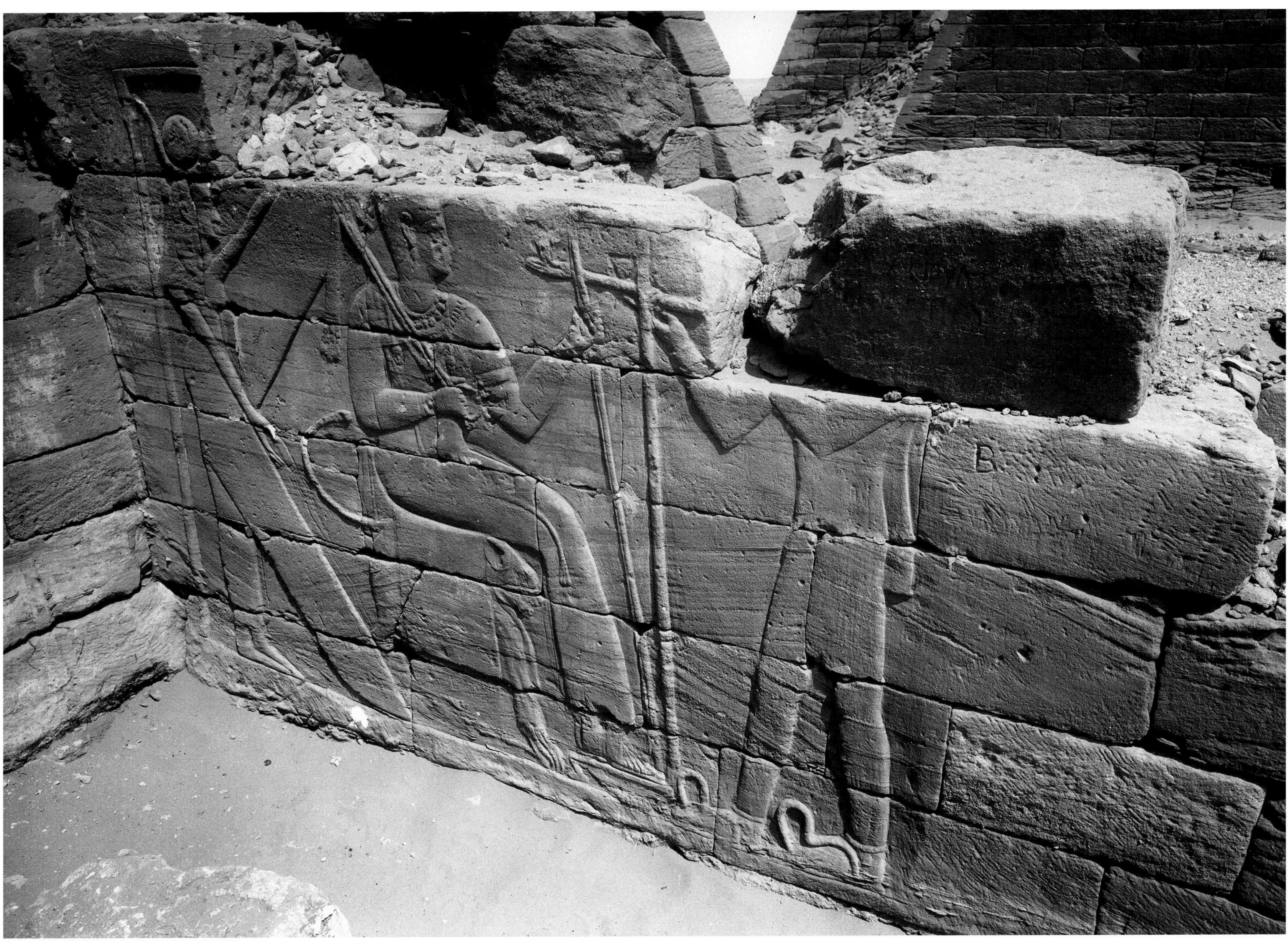

58
These sandstone statues show the god Amen of Napata as a ram protecting the king.
[Mohammedani Ibrahim Ibrahim]

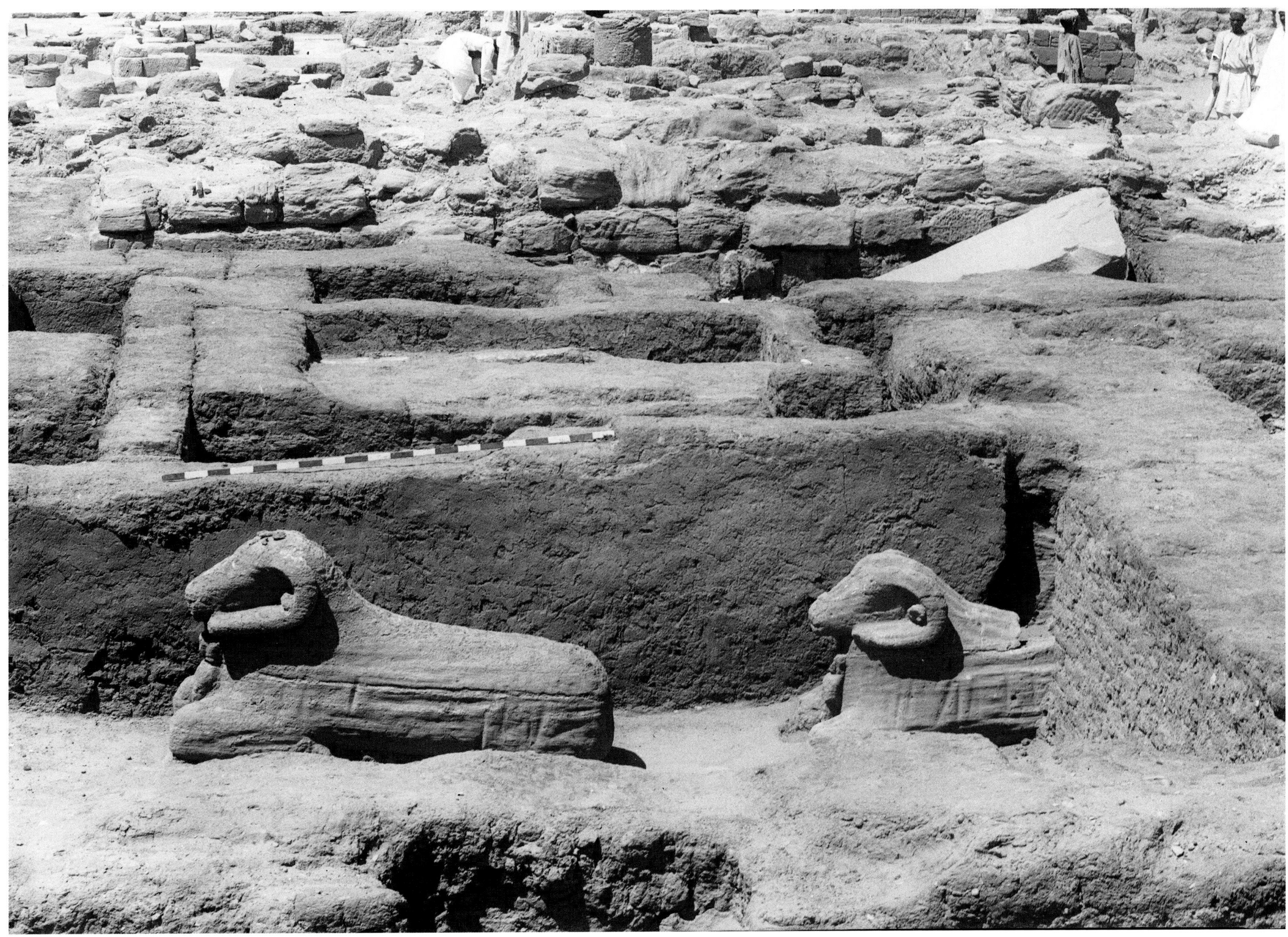

59

On December 16, 1913, the workers made a startling discovery, as recounted in the expedition's diary by Louis Caulton West: "I had just started breakfast when a man came running to say they had found a granite head—which later proved to be part of a life-sized seated female figure in absolute perfect condition except for surface cracks from the weather." This beautiful statue from the twentieth century BC, one of the great masterpieces of Egyptian art of the Twelfth Dynasty and a treasure of the MFA's Egyptian collection, was found in the largest of the royal tumuli at Kerma. It depicts Lady Sennuwy, the wife of the governor of the province of Asyut in southern Egypt. It probably came to Kerma as booty from a Nubian raid on Egypt. [Mohammedani Ibrahim Ibrahim]

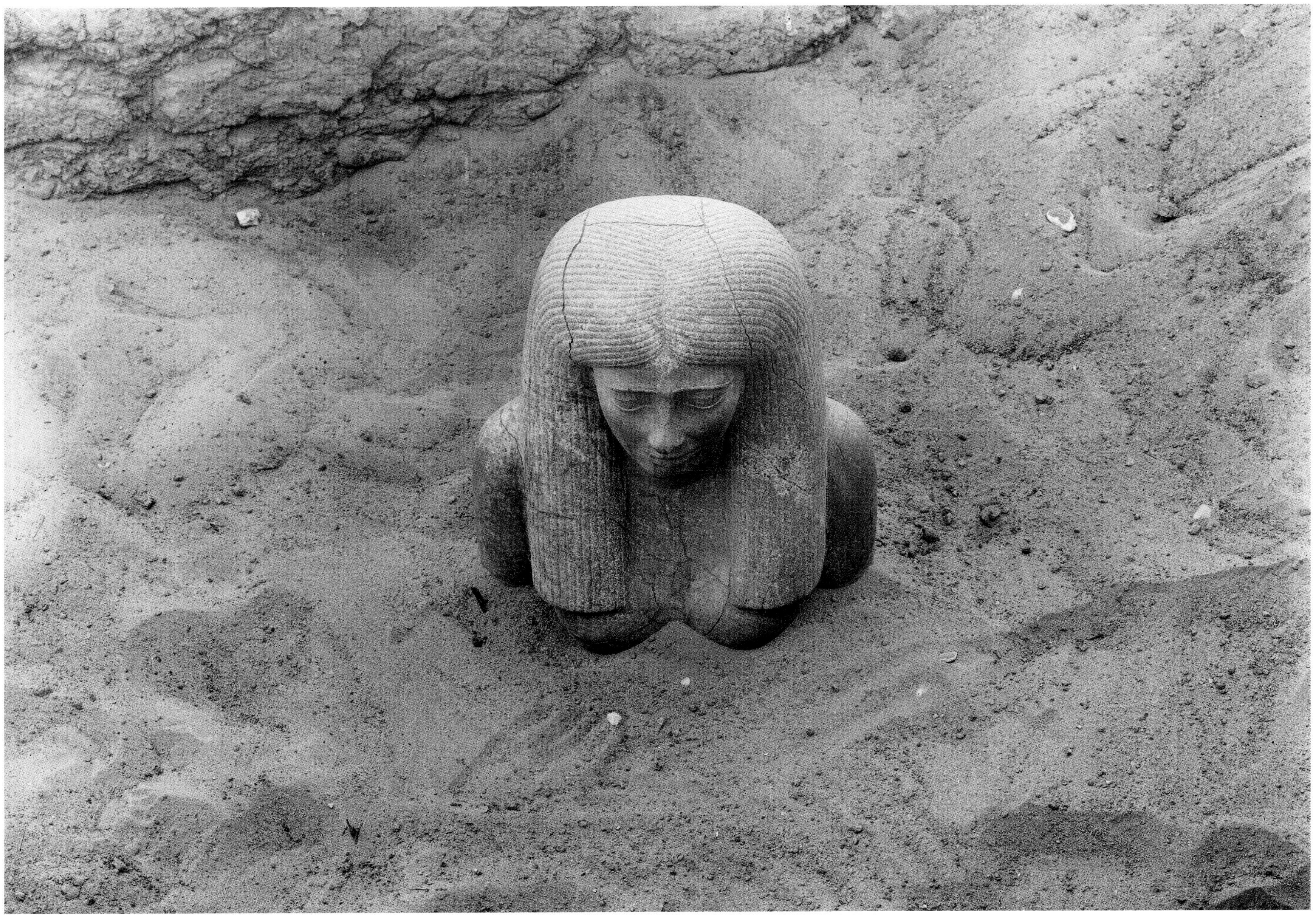

60
While searching for a place outside the temple proper to use as a dump, the expedition made
an extraordinary find: fragments of six over-life-size royal statues buried in a pit, including
a nearly complete statue of Aspelta. His body is seen from the back, lying on its side in the
foreground of the photograph. Plates 1 and 67 show the statue fragments reassembled.
[Mohammedani Ibrahim Ibrahim]

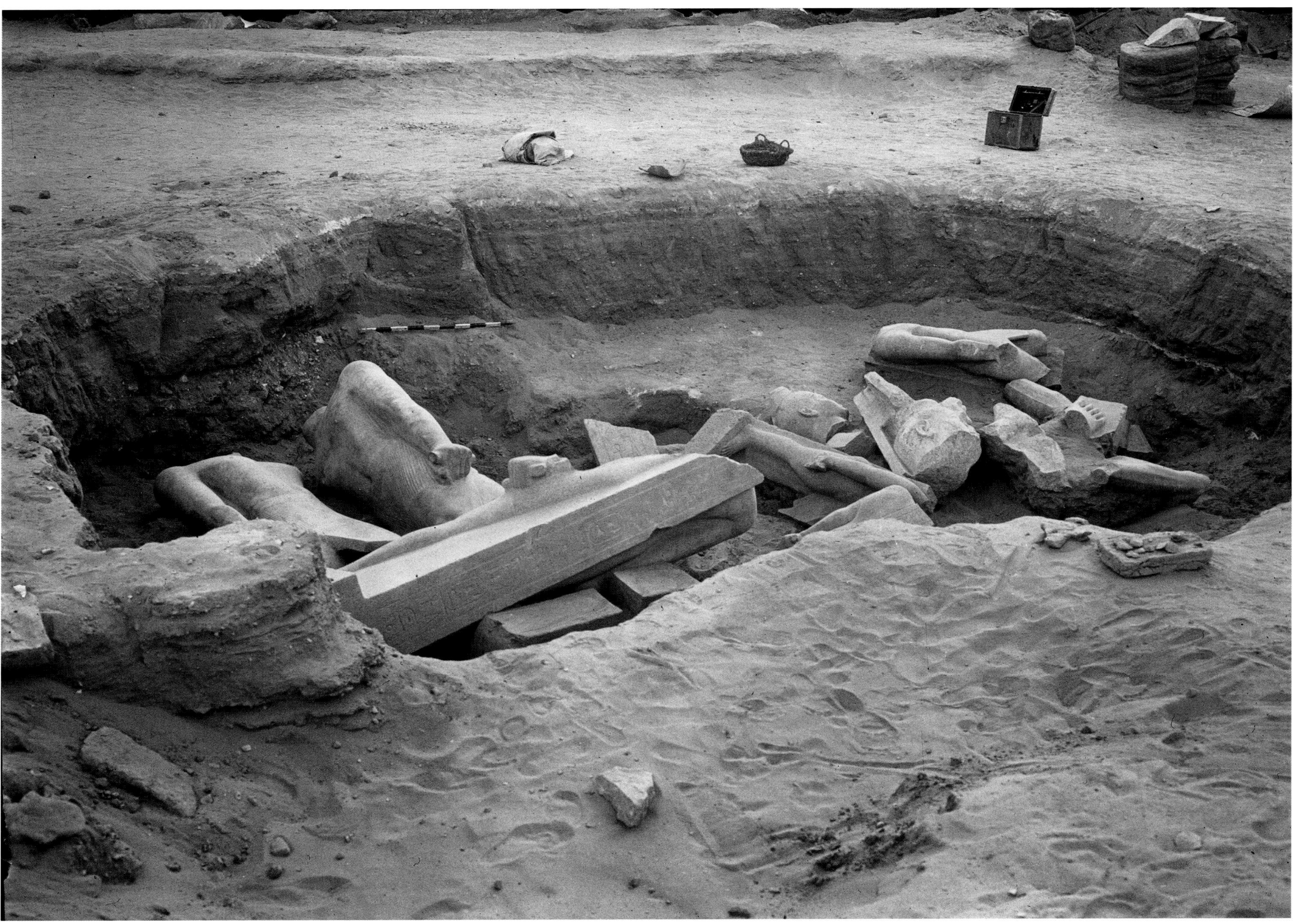

61
Six weeks later, a second cache of broken royal statues was found, and the fragments laid out on a cloth. From left to right: Tanwetamani (now in the Merowe Museum, Sudan), Senkamanisken (now in the Virginia Museum of Fine Arts), and another of Tanwetamani (now in the Toledo Museum of Art). [Mohammedani Ibrahim Ibrahim]

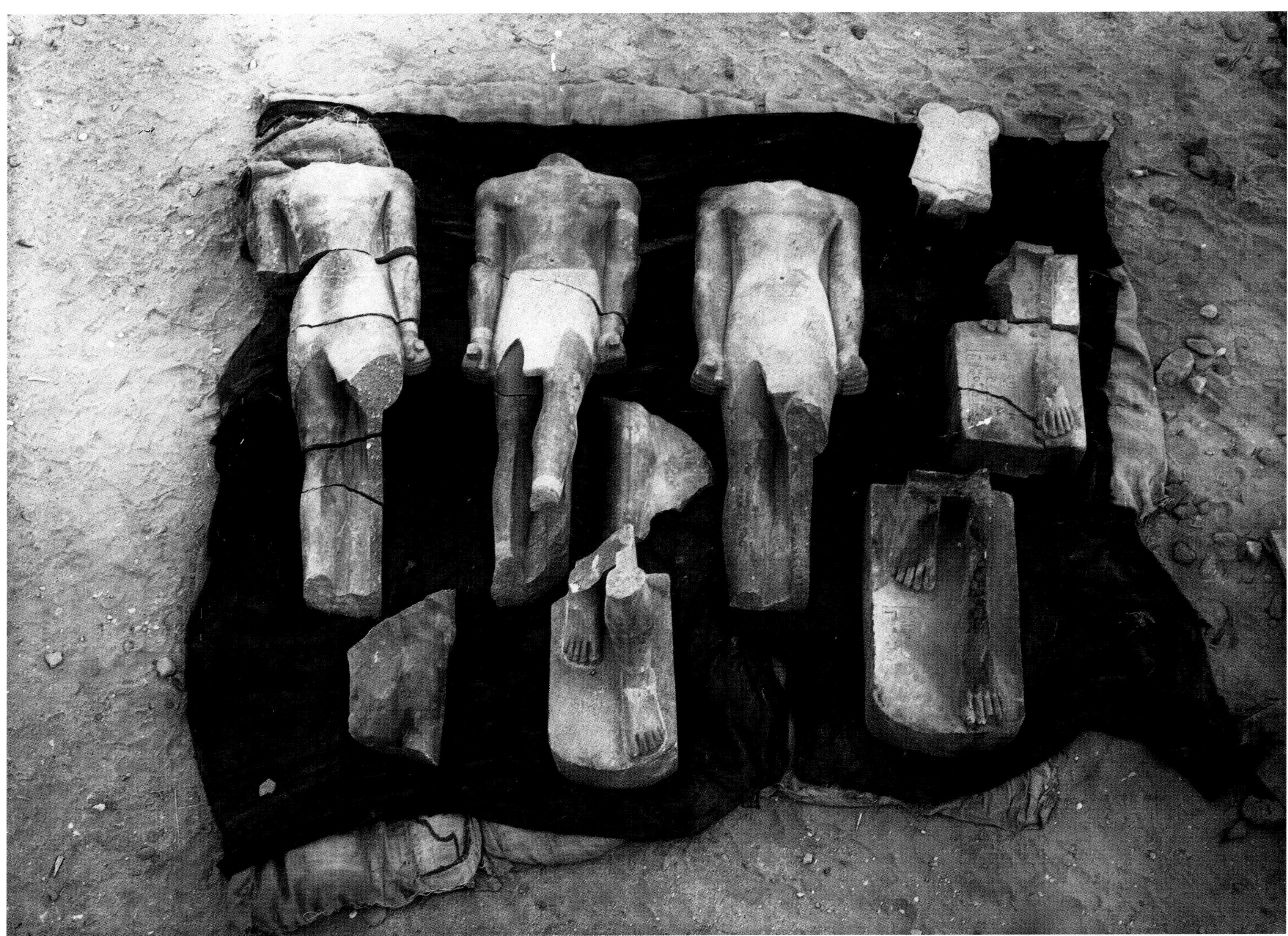

62

This head of a Nubian ruler was discovered three days before this photograph was taken, according
to Reisner's notation in the expedition diary: "In room 801, came on a granite head, lying face up.
Unfortunately the surfaces, especially chin, mouth, and nose, are crumbling to pieces as only granite
can crumble." Apparently the piece did not survive. This image and the diary entry appear to be
the only records of it. [Mohammedani Ibrahim Ibrahim]

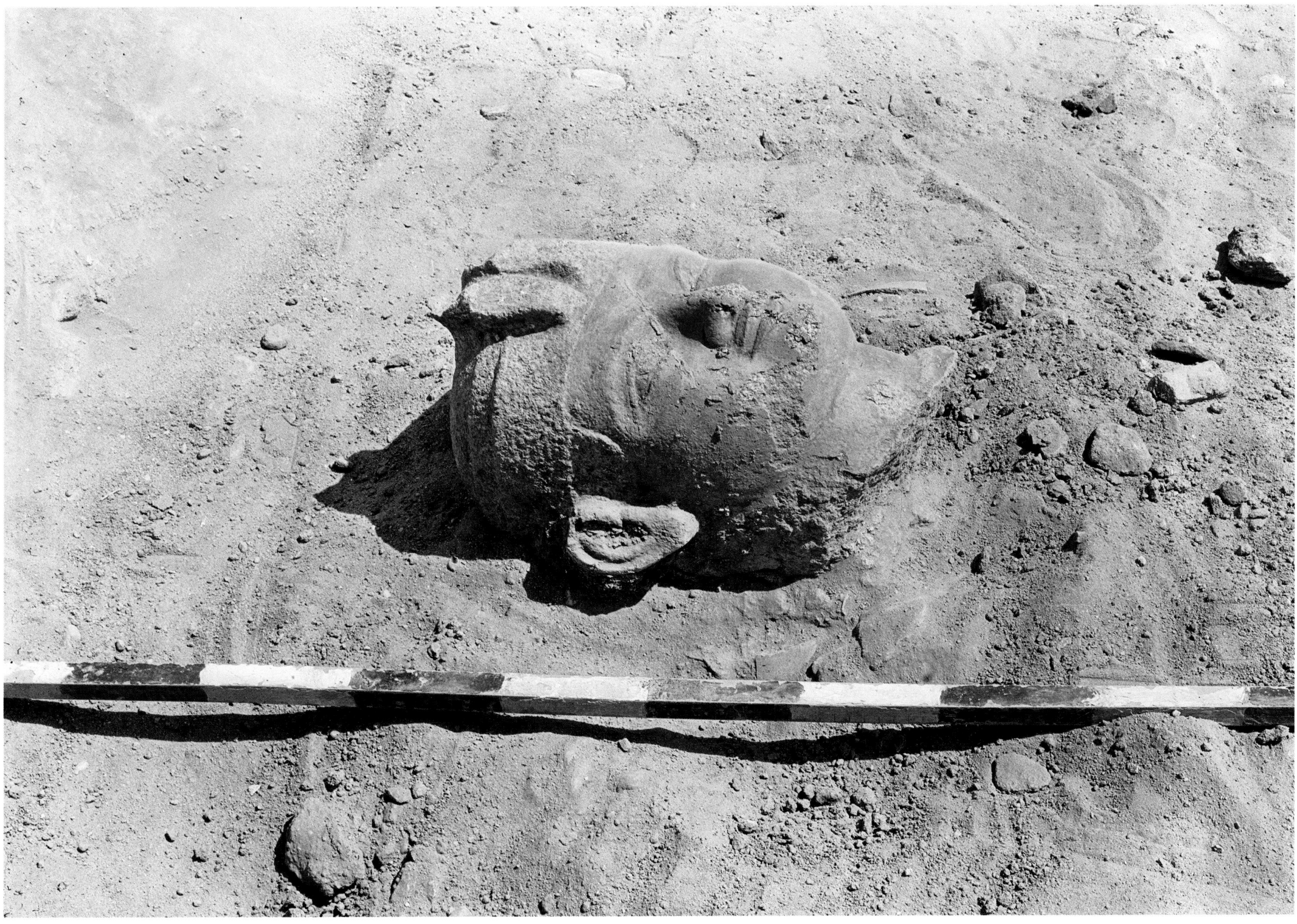

63

One custom in particular distinguished the burial practices at Kerma from Egyptian funerary rites of
the same period: At Kerma, rulers were accompanied in death by hundreds of sacrificial burials.
Later, members of the elite dug their graves into the great tumuli. These so-called subsidiary burials
also included sacrificial victims. The grave shown here contained at least twelve sacrificial burials.
[Mahmud Shadduf]

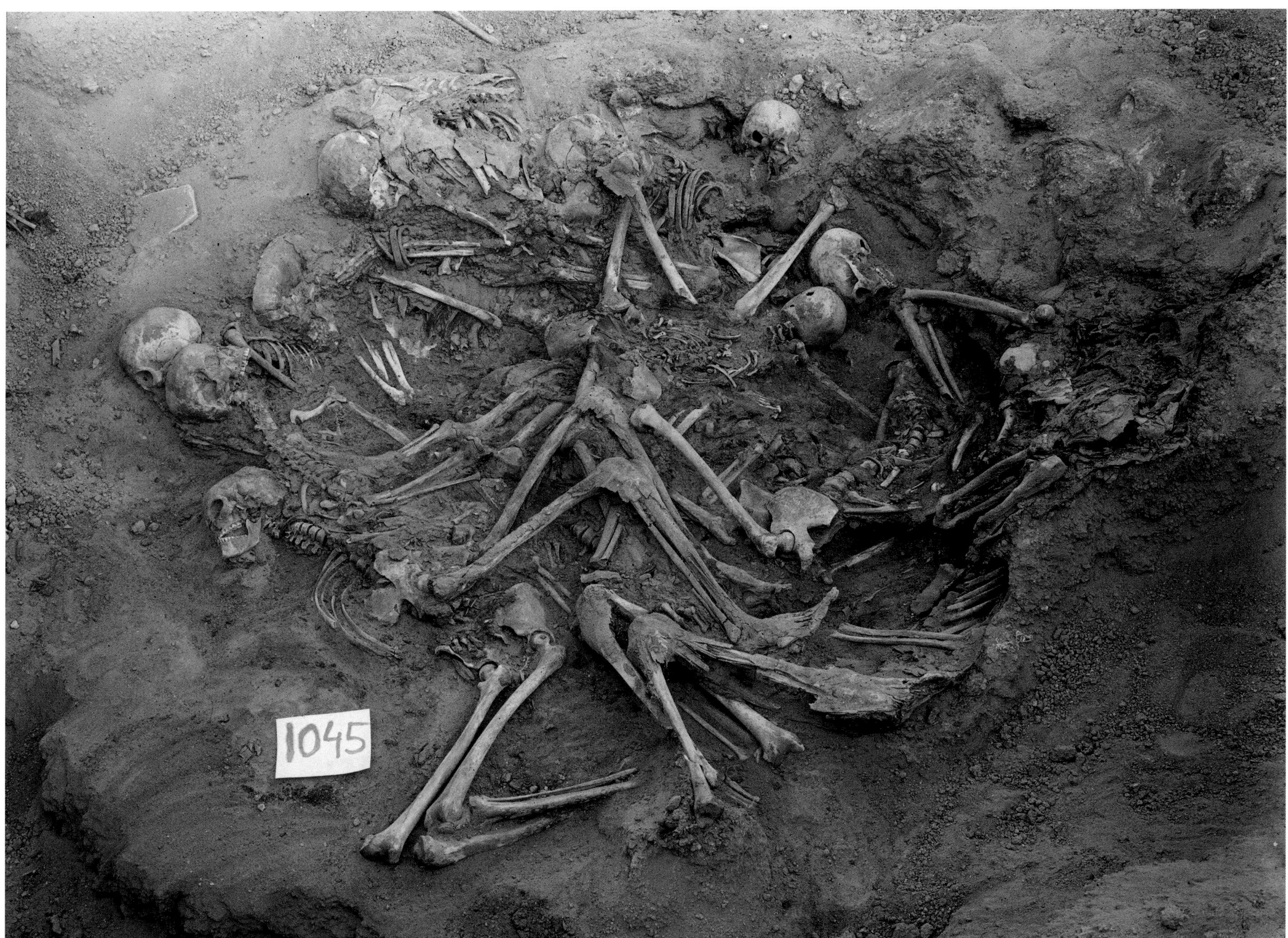
1045

64

The distinctive thin-walled "tulip beakers" found at Kerma were stacked and carried in woven net bags, as seen at left. [Mohammedani Ibrahim Ibrahim]

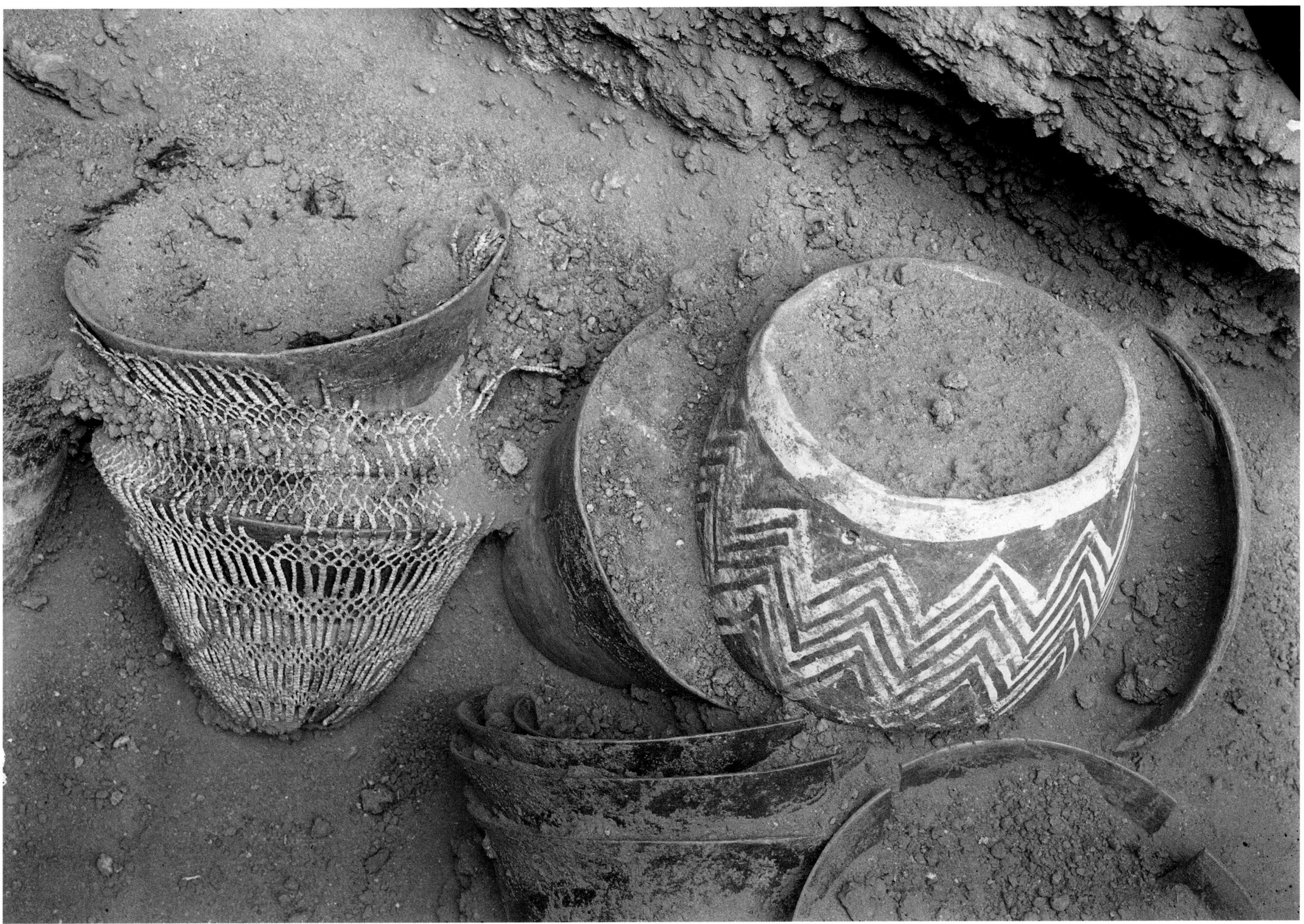

65
Large storage jars, as they were found in the burial chamber beneath one of the pyramids at Meroe.
[Mohammedani Ibrahim Ibrahim]

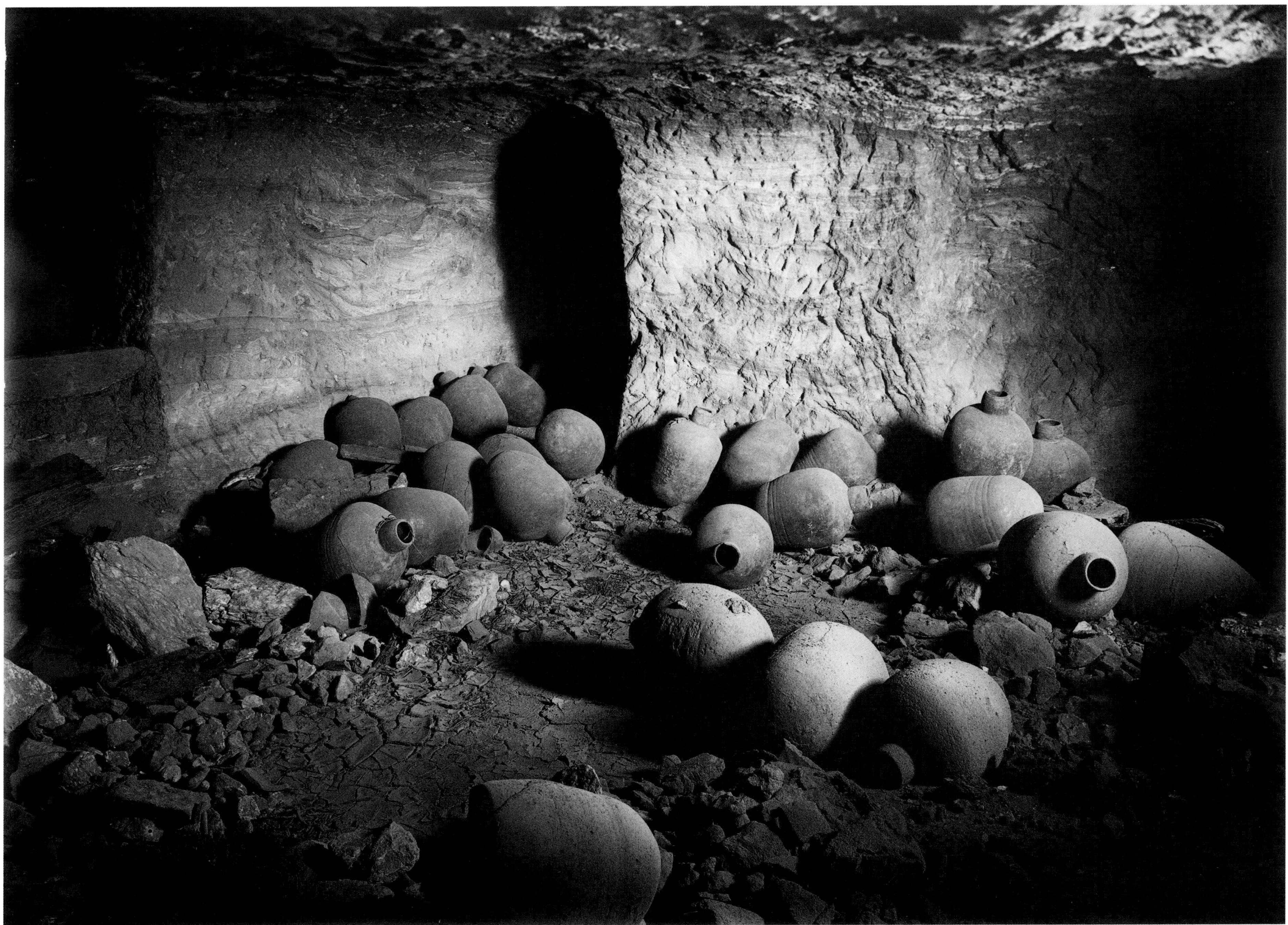

66

The excavation of the tomb of Taharqa in 1917 yielded an extraordinary number of stone funerary figurines (shawabties) in various sizes—1,107 in all. At the end of the season they were laid out on the sand beside the camp for sorting prior to packing. The pyramids of Nuri are in the background. [George Andrew Reisner]

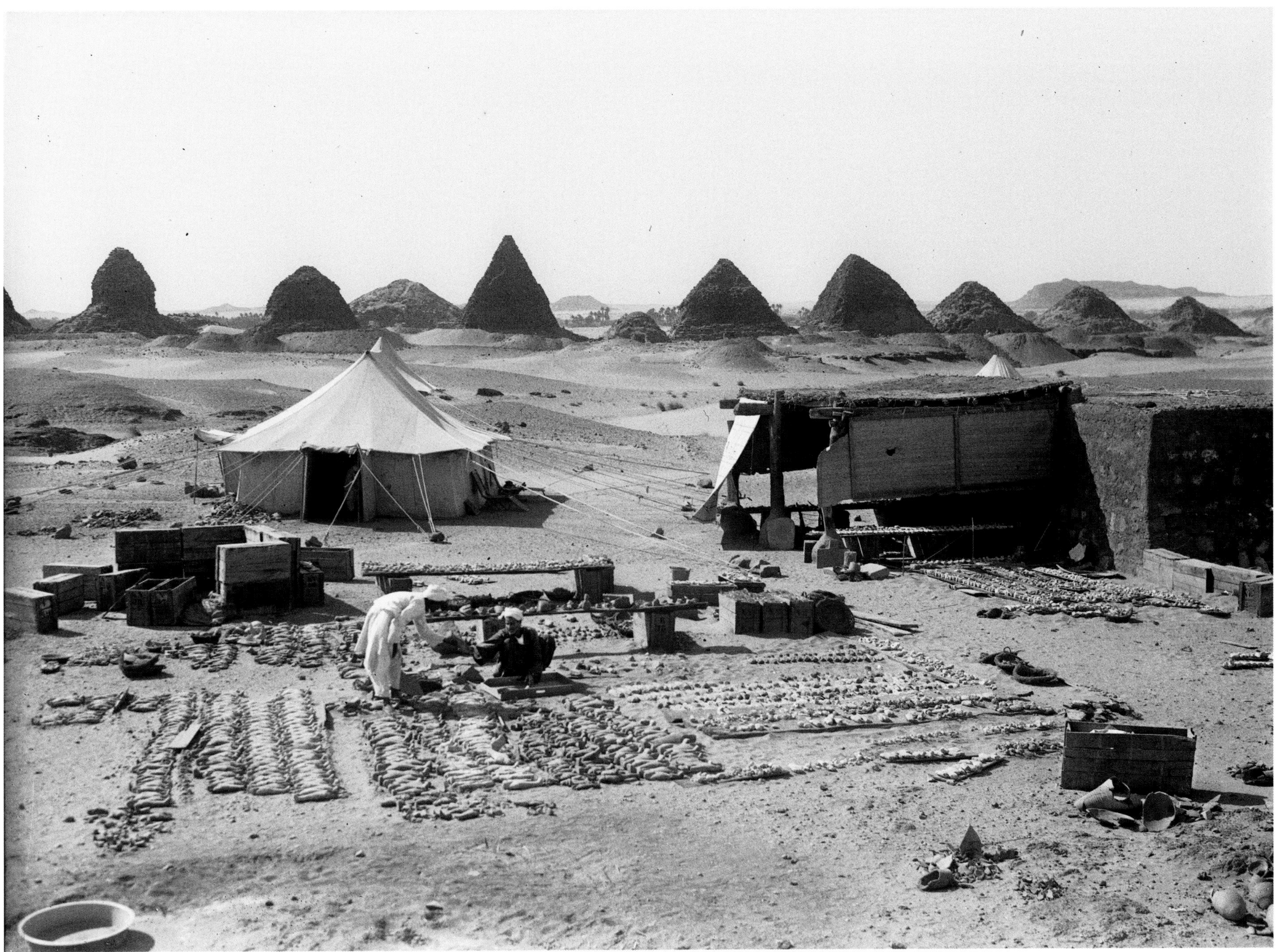

67

The colossal statue of Aspelta, completely assembled including its tall crown of feathers, stands
serenely and majestically before the camera. The atmosphere is quiet and calm, very different
from the bustle of the earlier scene (see plate 1). Only a bit of sleeve hints at the work involved in
staging and photographing the statue. [Mohammedani Ibrahim Ibrahim]

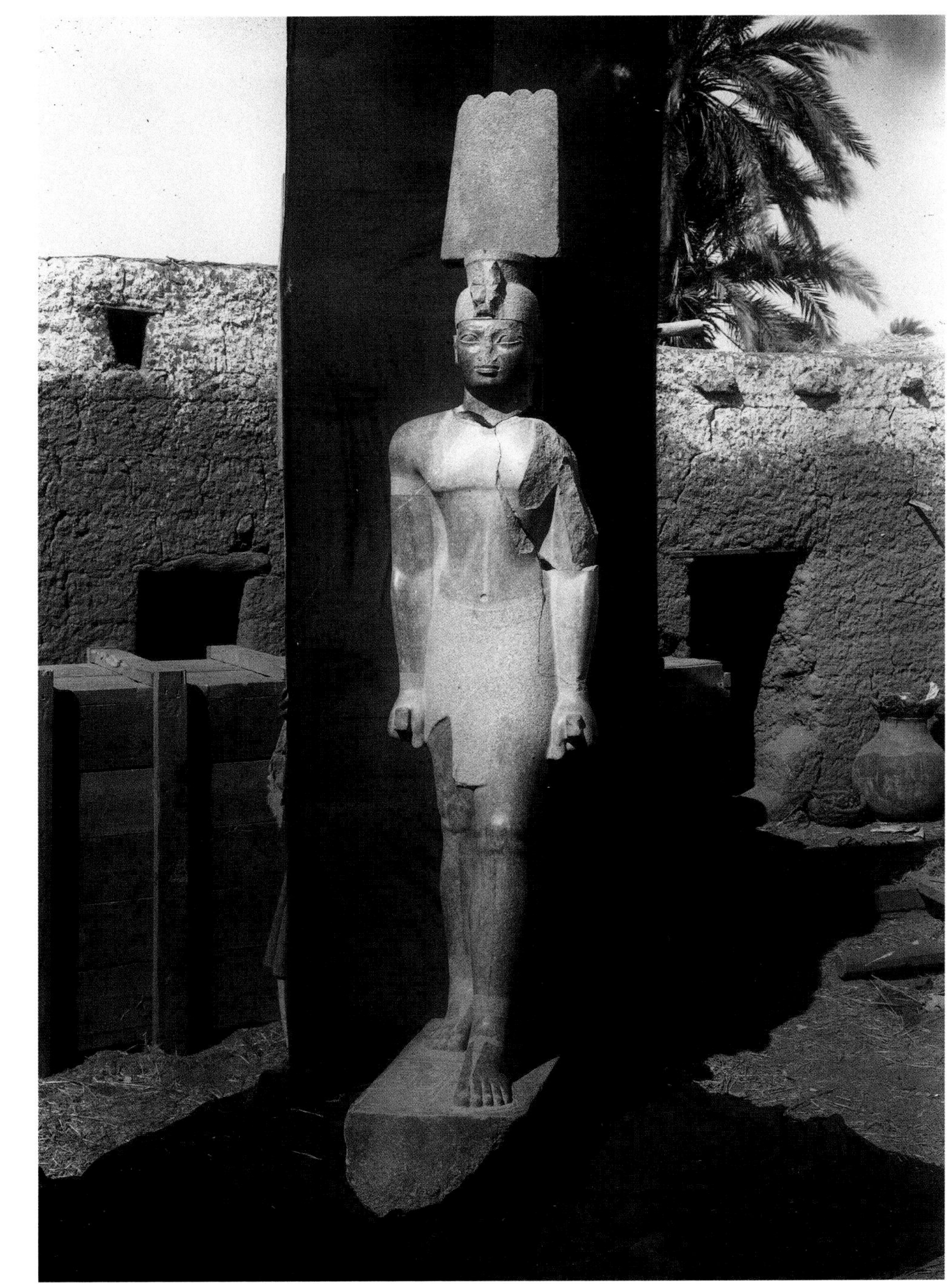

68
Boxes used at Uronarti camp to store small finds are arranged as a still life. [Mustapha Abu el-Hamd]

69 [overleaf]
Field Director Noel F. Wheeler and his wife pose languidly in the doorway of Kumma Temple.
He wears a pith helmet, jodhpurs, and puttees; she sports a sun hat and riding boots.
[Mustapha Abu el-Hamd]

70 [overleaf]
This photograph of Mrs. Wheeler outside the dig house was taken while the expedition was
excavating the fortress of Shalfak, a few miles north of Uronarti. [Mustapha Abu el-Hamd]

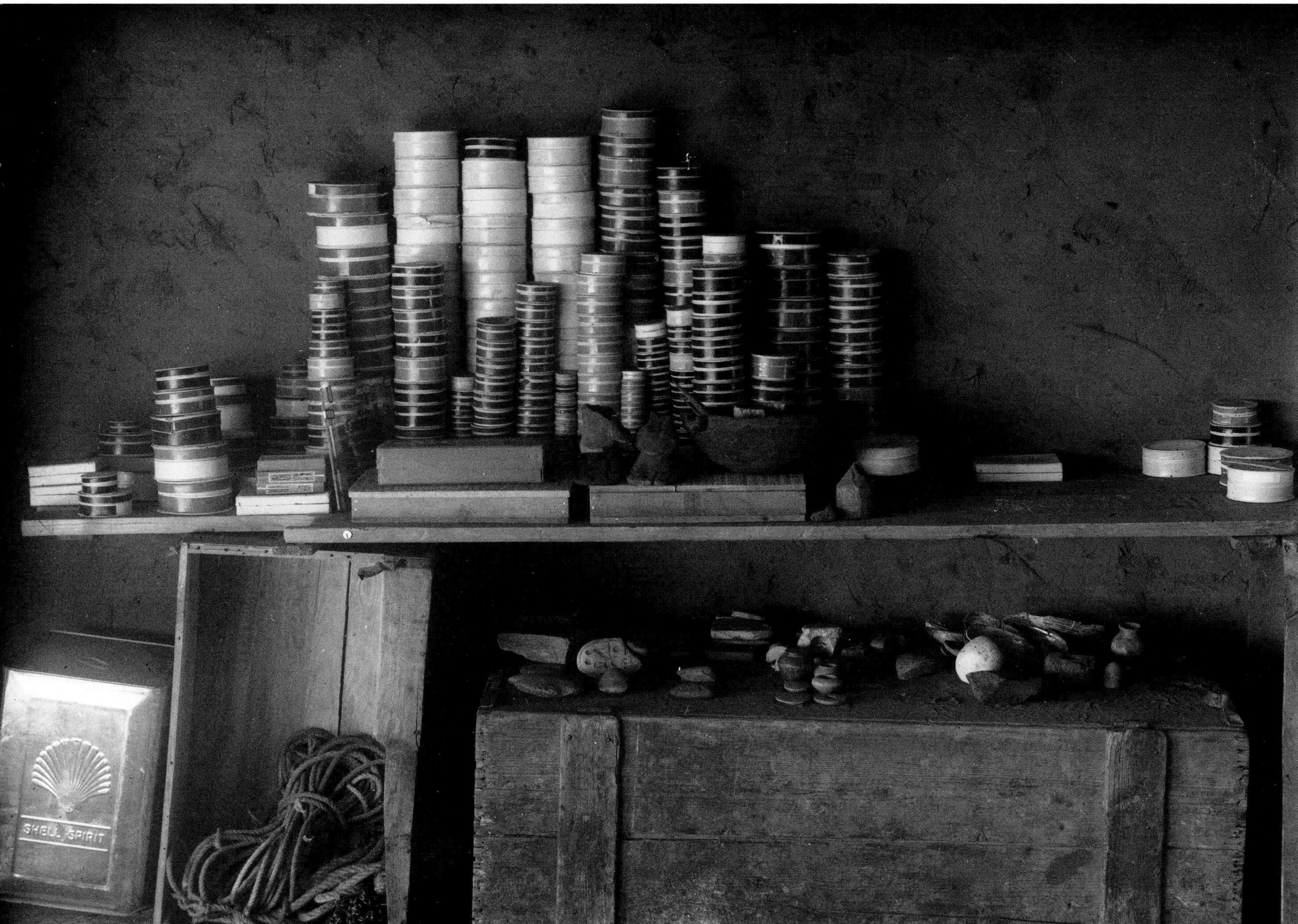

SHELL SPIRIT

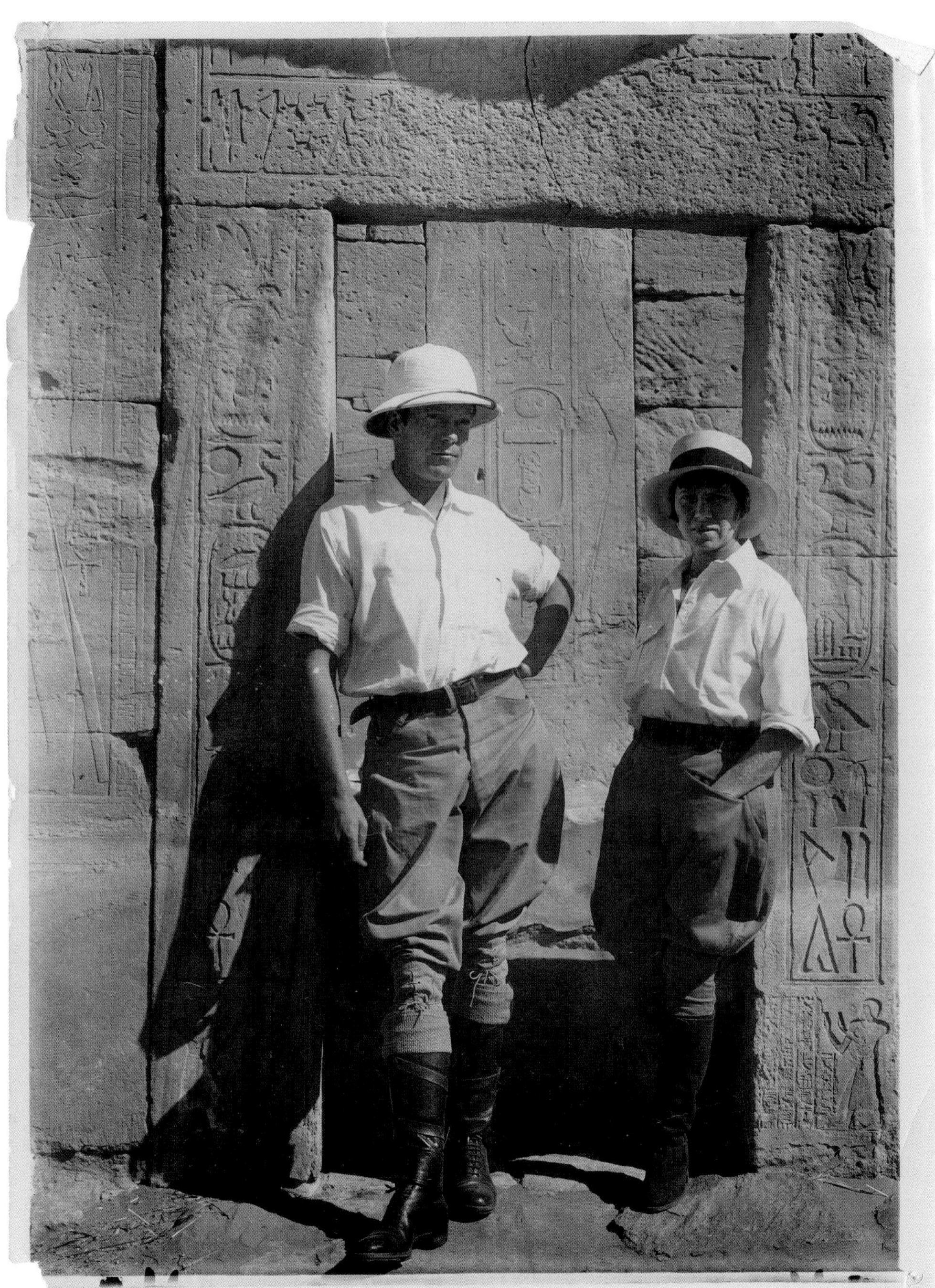

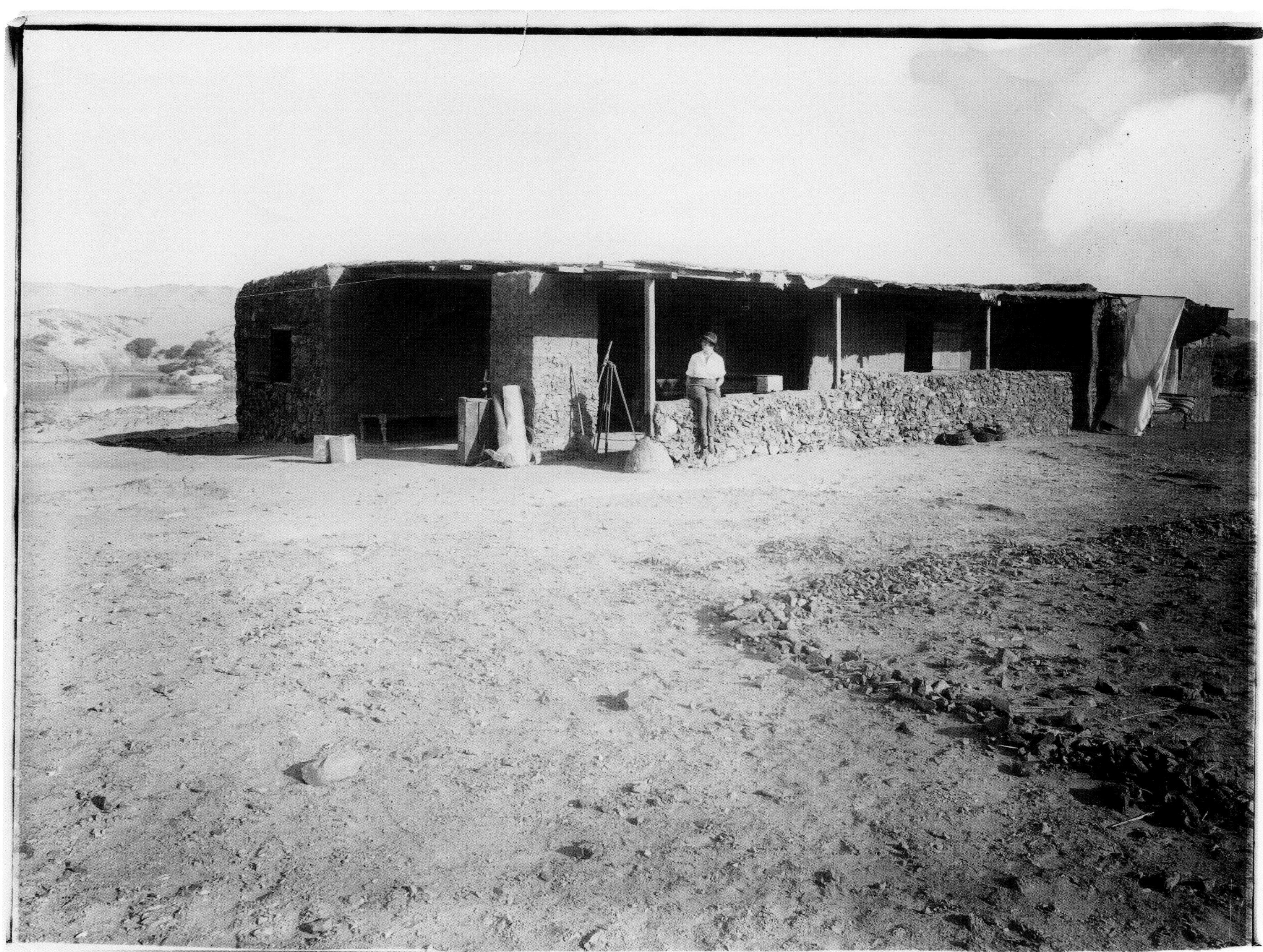

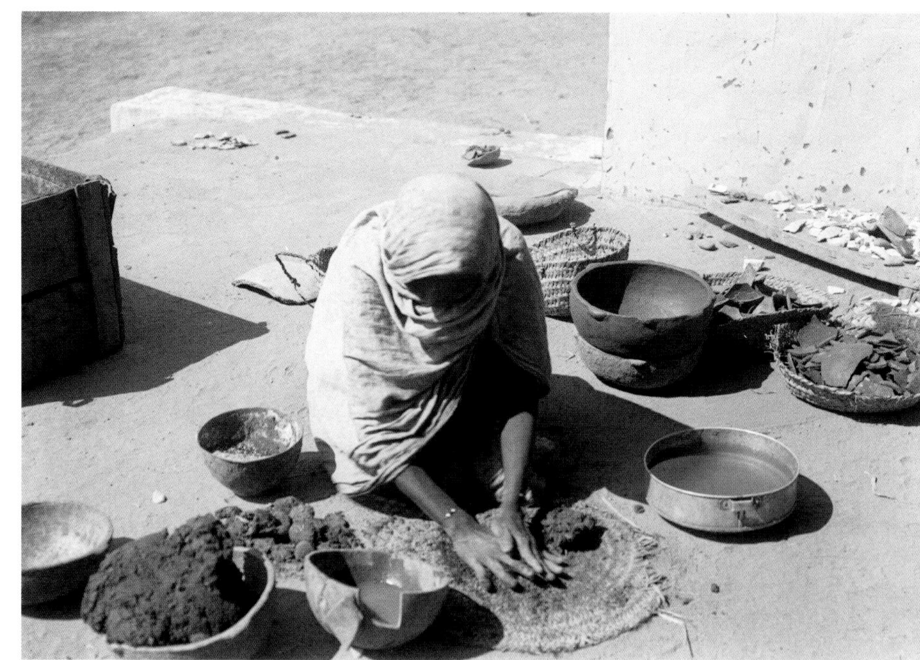

71–73

These photographs are from a series illustrating the process of pottery manufacture, in this case
a casserole or cooking vessel. The steps illustrated are: donkey dung being cut up for *tibn*
(straw temper for the clay); the potter hammering a hollow into the ball of clay; and applying
handles to the finished vessel. [Mahmud Shadduf]

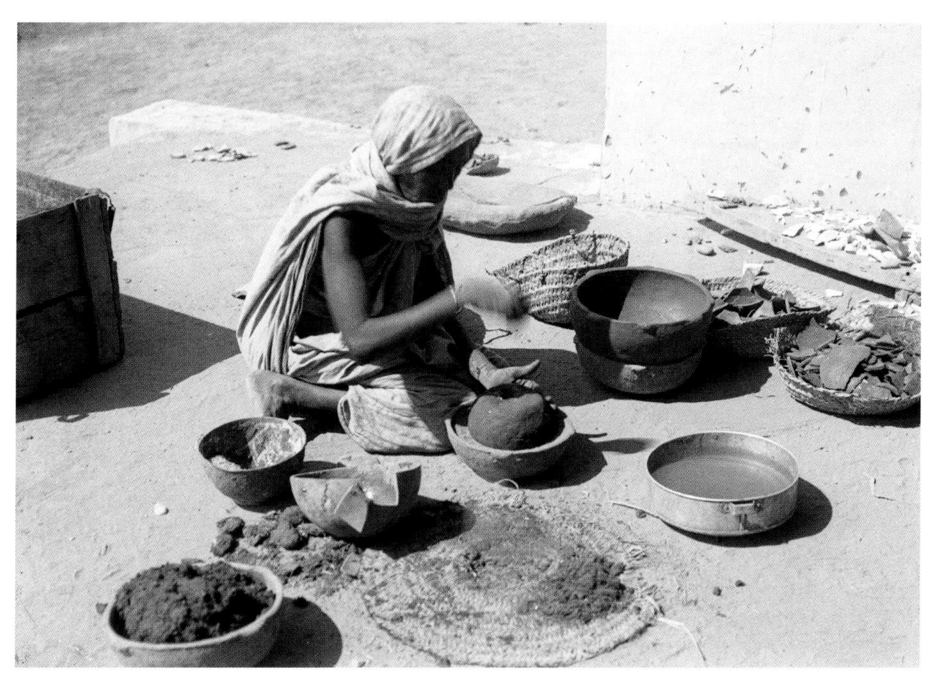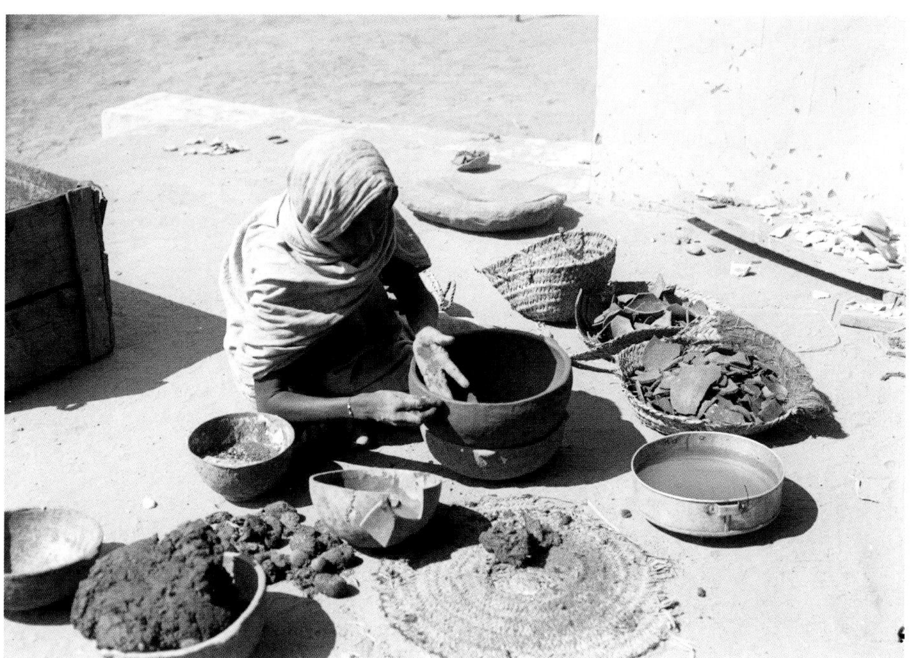

It's moving day. The expedition is leaving Barkal and moving camp to el-Kurru. Workers load the heavy equipment on a Sudanese boat, supervised by Mrs. Reisner, who is standing on board the government steamer *Waterlily*. The wooden table being loaded upside down is the same one that was set up as an outdoor workplace (see plate 39). [George Andrew Reisner]

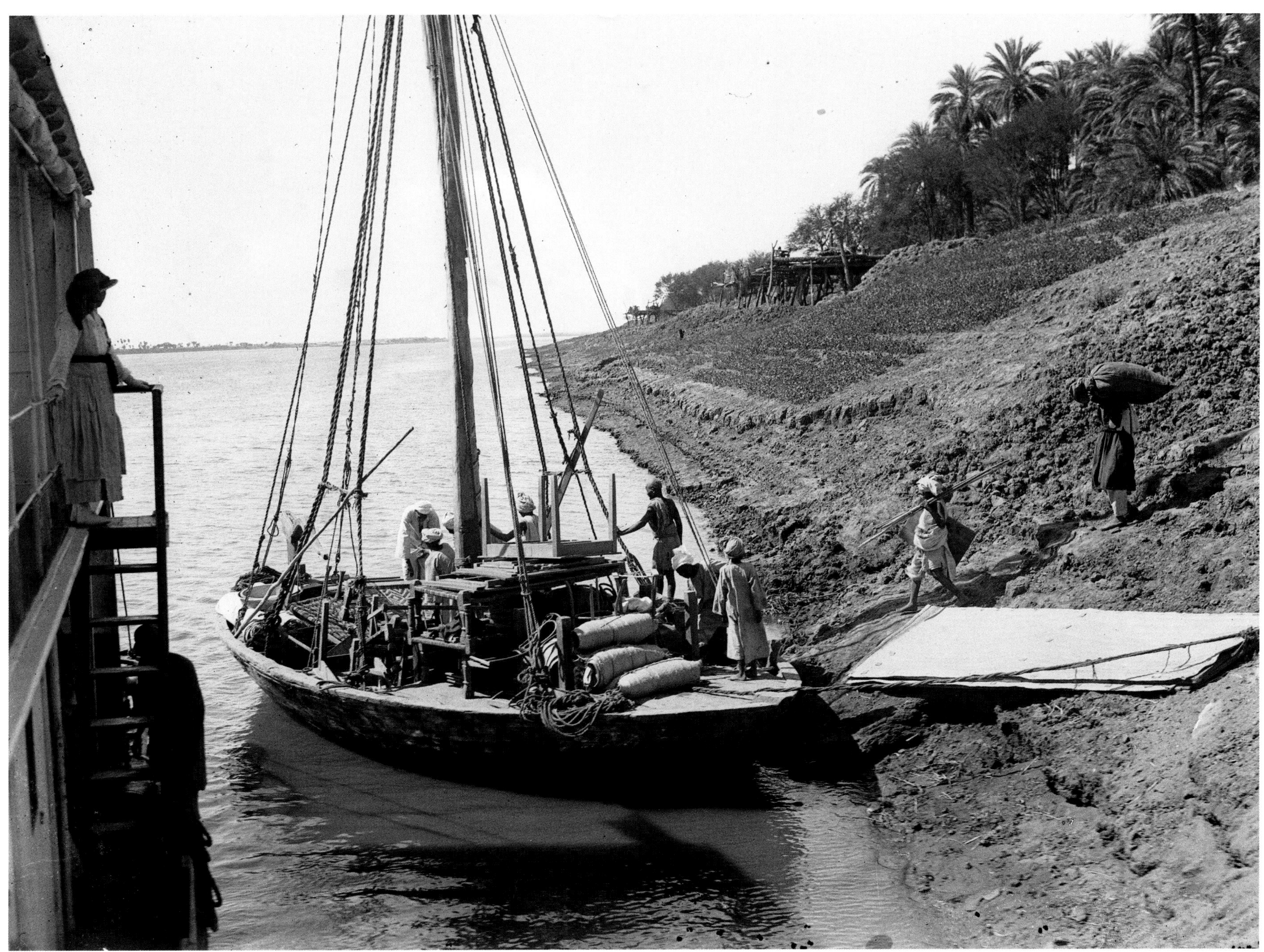

List of Illustrations

Images are digital positives made from glass-plate photographic negatives in the records of the Harvard University–Boston Museum of Fine Arts Expedition, housed at the Museum of Fine Arts, Boston, unless stated otherwise. Dimensions of plates whose identification numbers begin with A are 7 × 9 inches (about 18 × 23 cm); B, 5 × 7 inches (about 13 × 18 cm); C, 3 ½ × 4 ½ inches (about 9 × 11.5 cm); and D, 3 ¼ × 4 inches (about 9 × 10 cm).

1
Mohammedani Ibrahim Ibrahim
Gebel Barkal: Statue of Aspelta (MFA 23.730)
April 27, 1916
A2352_NS

2
Mohammedani Ibrahim Ibrahim
Giza: Expedition staff with MFA president George H. Edgell and George Reisner at Harvard Camp
February 26, 1938
A7924PA_NS

3
George Andrew Reisner
Giza: Front of Harvard Camp, Mohammed Shadduf contact-printing glass-plate negatives on printing-out paper through direct exposure to sunlight, with puppy "Patrick Cheops"
November 20, 1916
D109_NS

4
Plate 21 from Dows Dunham, *The Barkal Temples* (Boston: Museum of Fine Arts, 1970)

5
Mohammedani Ibrahim Ibrahim
Semna: Semna Fort with Kumma in background, looking upstream
February 3, 1923
A3275_NS

6
Mustapha Abu el-Hamd
Uronarti: Southeast wing of the fort, south wall with mudbrick buttresses
December 15, 1928
A4993_NS

7
Mohammedani Ibrahim Ibrahim
Semna: Thutmose III temple, southwest corner
May 2, 1924
B5350_NS

8
Mustapha Abu el-Hamd
Second Cataract viewed from the western shore at Semna
November 6, 1928
A4957_NS

9
Mustapha Abu el-Hamd
Second Cataract at Semna,
date boats returning
November 16, 1928
B6608_NS

10
Mustapha Abu el-Hamd
Uronarti Fort from the eastern bank
January 9, 1929
C11651_NS

11
Mahmud Shadduf
Kerma: Western Deffufa
February 13, 1913
A916_NS

12
Mohammedani Ibrahim Ibrahim
Kerma: Tumuli XVII, XVIII, XIX
January 8, 1914
B2132_NS

13
Mohammedani Ibrahim Ibrahim
Kerma: Tumulus IV, partially excavated
January 13, 1914
A2008_NS

14
Mohammedani Ibrahim Ibrahim
Nuri: Pyramids from the southeast
May 1, 1917
A2655_NS

15
Mohammedani Ibrahim Ibrahim
Nuri: Pyramids from the top of Pyramid 12
(Amanineteyerike)
May 1, 1917
A2658_NS

16
Mohammedani Ibrahim Ibrahim
Begrawiya: North Cemetery at Meroe
April 2, 1921
A3053_NS

17
Mohammedani Ibrahim Ibrahim
Begrawiya: North Cemetery at Meroe,
Pyramids N 32 and N 19
April 12, 1921
A3056_NS

18
Mohammedani Ibrahim Ibrahim
Gebel Barkal: Pyramids 1–8
May 19, 1920
B3798_NS

19
Mohammedani Ibrahim Ibrahim
Gebel Barkal: Pyramid 4
February 18, 1916
A2358_NS

20
Mohammedani Ibrahim Ibrahim
Nuri: Pyramid 6 (Anlamani),
east face and end of stair
November 15, 1916
B2862_NS

21
Mohammedani Ibrahim Ibrahim
Nuri: Pyramid 6 (Anlamani), with workers
November 15, 1916
C7338_NS

22
Mohammedani Ibrahim Ibrahim
Gebel Barkal: Pyramid 3
February 19, 1916
B2664_NS

23
Mohammedani Ibrahim Ibrahim
Gebel Barkal: Pyramid 11, stair from room A
February 19, 1916
B2660_NS

24
Mohammedani Ibrahim Ibrahim
Nuri: Pyramid 52 (a queen), end of entrance stair
seen through doorway from Room A
January 4, 1918
C8184_NS

25
Mahmud Shadduf
El-Kurru: Pyramid 16, Room B
March 12, 1919
A2766_NS

26
Mahmud Shadduf
El-Kurru: Pyramid 18, Room B
March 31, 1919
B3651_NS

27
Mahmud Shadduf
Nuri: Pyramid 8 (Aspelta), Room A
April 25, 1918
C8521_NS

28
Mohammedani Ibrahim Ibrahim
Nuri: Pyramid 8 (Aspelta), Room A, Reisner,
Dunham, Tai Mohamed, Ahmed (M.)
cleaning gold cylinders on floor
April 20, 1916
B2777_NS

29
Mohammedani Ibrahim Ibrahim
Nuri: Mr. Williams on raft in
Pyramid 1 (Taharqa),
entrance to burial chamber
March 30, 1917
C7710_NS

30
Mohammedani Ibrahim Ibrahim
Nuri: Pyramid 6 (Anlamani),
men at work getting out the sarcophagus
of King Anlamani
April 12, 1917
D366_NS

31
Mohammedani Ibrahim Ibrahim
Nuri: Pyramid 6 (Anlamani), workers
transporting sarcophagus
April 18, 1917
D386_NS

32
Mohammedani Ibrahim Ibrahim
Nuri: Sarcophagus from Pyramid 6 (Anlamani)
May 6, 1917
A2651_NS

33
Mohammedani Ibrahim Ibrahim
Nuri: Sarcophagus lid from Pyramid 6 (Anlamani)
May 5, 1917
A2650_NS

34
Mohammedani Ibrahim Ibrahim
Gebel Barkal: View of mountain with
Great Temple of Amen at its foot
May 4, 1921
A3078_NS

35
Mahmud Shadduf
Gebel Barkal: Great Temple of Amen
from top of Gebel Barkal
January 27, 1919
A2744_NS

36
Mahmud Shadduf
Gebel Barkal: Temple of Mut (B 300),
Hathor columns of Taharqa
January 30, 1919
C8630_NS

37
Mohammedani Ibrahim Ibrahim
Nuri: Visit of Reisner to Pyramid 3 (Senkamanisken);
from right to left, Mary Reisner, Mrs. Reisner,
Mrs. Symons
February 19, 1917
B2992_NS

38
Mohammedani Ibrahim Ibrahim
Gebel Barkal: George Reisner entertaining Governor
William Jackson Pasha in Temple of Atlanersa (B 700),
rooms 703 and 704
March 17, 1916
B2714_NS

39
Mahmud Shadduf
Gebel Barkal: Great Temple of Amen
(B 500), room 503, middle aisle with work table
January 20, 1919
C8616_NS

40
Mohammedani Ibrahim Ibrahim
Gebel Barkal: George Reisner taking
survey measurements
B 801 and B 802
March 2, 1920
C9012_NS

41
Mohammedani Ibrahim Ibrahim
Nuri: Pyramid 7 (Karkamani),
workers carrying debris out of pyramid,
rising from the stairway
January 15, 1917
C7422_NS

42
Mohammedani Ibrahim Ibrahim
Gebel Barkal: Local workers lined up at Reisner's tent
March 30, 1916
C7170_NS

43
Mohammedani Ibrahim Ibrahim
Begrawiya: Boy with rope and water bag
February 4, 1922
D733_NS

44
Mohammedani Ibrahim Ibrahim
Nuri: Women and children waiting with
food for workers
January 14, 1917
C7414_NS

45
Mohammedani Ibrahim Ibrahim
Nuri: Young girl carrying food, wearing large
amulet and beads
February 24, 1917
B3010_NS

46
Mohammedani Ibrahim Ibrahim
Kerma: Men baking bread
March 12, 1914
C6153_NS

47
Mahmud Shadduf
Kerma: Beads and pendants: faience, amethyst, glazed
crystal, carnelian, shell, garnet, granite (includes MFA
14.1416, 14.1546, 20.1715, 20.1719, 20.1728)
August 10, 1914, Giza Camp
A2130_NS

48
Bedawi Ahmed Abu Bukr
Begrawiya, West Cemetery: amulets and other objects
from various tombs (includes gold amulet of Bastet,
MFA 23.335)
March 19, 1923
A3151_NS

49
Mahmud Shadduf
Kerma: Ostrich-feather fan (MFA 13.4198)
July 1, 1913, Giza Camp
B1992_NS

50
Mohammedani Ibrahim Ibrahim
Ivory inlays (includes MFA 20.1505, 20.1530, 20.1540,
20.1541, 20.1543a-d, 20.1544, 20.2100)
February 9, 1914
A2035_NS

51
Mahmud Shadduf
Kerma: Copper sheet lion inlays
September 9, 1914, Giza Camp
A2158_NS

52
Mahmud Shadduf
Kerma: Assorted objects of wood, bronze,
hematite, and ivory (includes MFA 13.4006, 13.4007,
13.4010, 13.4012, 13.4013, 13.4014, 13.4016)
April 1, 1913
A927_NS

53
Mahmud Shadduf
Kerma: Mass of green glazed crystal beads
August 6, 1914, Giza Camp
B2239_NS

54
Mohammedani Ibrahim Ibrahim
Nuri: Pyramid 59 (Queen Malakaye): three pairs of inlay
eyes from coffins (MFA 21.855a-b, 21.856a-b, 21.857a-b)
April 19, 1918
C8501_NS

55
Mohammedani Ibrahim Ibrahim
Begrawiya: Pyramid N 5, Room A: bronze statue fragments
(includes MFA 24.896, 24.897)
May 30, 1923, Giza Camp
B4531_NS

56
Mohammedani Ibrahim Ibrahim
Begrawiya: Pyramid N 18, Room A, bronze "centaur" lamp
March 10, 1923
B4440_NS

57
Mohammedani Ibrahim Ibrahim
Gebel Barkal: Pyramid 4, reliefs inside chapel
February 19, 1916
A2319_NS

58
Mohammedani Ibrahim Ibrahim
Gebel Barkal: B 850, sandstone sphinxes
February 28, 1920
C9001_NS

59
Mohammedani Ibrahim Ibrahim
Kerma: Statue of Lady Sennuwy emerging (MFA 14.720)
December 16, 1913
B2119_NS

60
Mohammedani Ibrahim Ibrahim
Gebel Barkal: Trench in Temple B 500, fragments
of statues in situ
February 27, 1916
B2680_NS

61
Mohammedani Ibrahim Ibrahim
Gebel Barkal: Statues (headless) of Tanwetamani
and Senkamanisken
May 1, 1916
A2356_NS

62
Mohammedani Ibrahim Ibrahim
Gebel Barkal: Temple B 800, room 801,
head of a Nubian ruler
April 3, 1916
C7188_NS

63
Mahmud Shadduf
Kerma: Grave K 1045
March 25, 1913
C4397_NS

64
Mohammedani Ibrahim Ibrahim
Kerma: Pottery, painted vessel, and stacks of Kerma
beakers, some still with woven carrying nets
December 27, 1913
C5865_NS

65
Mohammedani Ibrahim Ibrahim
Begrawiya: Pyramid N 17, room A, showing pottery in situ
April 1, 1921
A3051_NS

66
George Andrew Reisner
Nuri: Camp, showing shawabties laid out
March 19, 1917
D335_NS

67
Mohammedani Ibrahim Ibrahim
Gebel Barkal: Statue of Aspelta (MFA 23.730)
April 24, 1920
A2986_NS

68
Mustapha Abu el-Hamd
Uronarti: Containers for storage of small objects
December 24, 1928
C11619_NS

69
Mustapha Abu el-Hamd
Kumma: Lt. Com. Noel Wheeler and Mrs. Wheeler
December 12, 1928
Photographic print
B6652_NS

70
Mustapha Abu el-Hamd
Shalfak: Harvard Camp at Sarras/Shalfak
with Mrs. Noel Wheeler
March 1, 1931
Photographic print
A6209_NS

71
Mahmud Shadduf
Kerma: Modern pot making, cutting up
donkey dung for *tibn* (straw temper)
March 1, 1913
C4298_NS

72
Mahmud Shadduf
Kerma: Modern pot making, hammering
hollow in ball of prepared clay with fist
March 1, 1913
C4300_NS

73
Mahmud Shadduf
Kerma: Modern pot making, applying
handles to finished vessel
March 1, 1913
C4305_NS

74
George Andrew Reisner
Gebel Barkal: Native boat loaded with
camp stuff alongside steamer *Waterlily*
at Barkal, Mrs. Reisner at left
February 21, 1919
D557_NS

—

Details
pages 2-3: plate 41
page 4: plate 54
page 11: plate 39

Acknowledgments

This book grew out of a much larger project. The MFA houses some forty-five thousand glass-plate negatives documenting forty years of work by the Harvard University–Boston Museum of Fine Arts Expedition at twenty-three sites in Egypt and Sudan. For years now the Museum has been digitizing these glass plates for preservation and ease of access. From 2001 to 2004, the roughly twenty thousand negatives from Giza were scanned as part of the Giza Archives project, funded by the Andrew W. Mellon Foundation. In 2010 we turned to the plates from the excavations in northern Sudan, roughly ten thousand photographs documenting work at eleven sites from 1913 to 1932. It was my task to pull the plates batch by batch from the metal cabinets in which they are stored and take them to the photo studio to be scanned.

I was already familiar with many of the images from their publication in the excavation reports and various scholarly articles, as well as from my own research in the departmental archives. A number of images had been included in our gallery labels to illustrate the archaeological context of the works on display. I was struck particularly by the many images of work in progress or of expedition personnel that had never made it into print, and by the wealth of information contained in the original photographs.

The idea for the book came out of discussions with the publications department here at the Museum. Rather than telling the story of the excavations or illustrating a trip up the Nile, we chose to focus on the photographs themselves and the stories behind them— stories not so much about the excavations in progress as about the process of excavation. Emiko K. Usui, the former director of MFA Publications, supported the project with enthusiasm, as has her colleague Anna K. Barnet. I am most grateful to my editor, Jennifer Snodgrass, who encouraged me to think outside the box, mixing sites for the sake of the visual narrative. Anne Levine, Terry McAweeney, and Hope Stockton moved production of the book forward. Designer Daphne Geismar immediately grasped our intentions and came up with a sleek and elegant layout.

Matthew Teitelbaum, Ann and Graham Gund Director, and Katie Getchell, Chief Brand Officer and Deputy Director, saw the appeal these images would have to a wider public.

In my own department of Art of the Ancient World, I thank Rita E. Freed, John F. Cogan Jr. and Mary L. Cornille Chair; Denise Doxey, Curator, Ancient Egyptian, Nubian, and Near Eastern Art; and above all, Susan Allen, Research Associate for Egyptian Expedition Archives. Susan took over the task of working with the photograph registers, helped with the selection of images, and gladly shared her knowledge of archaeological practice and historical archives. Her own work with Harry Burton's photographic record of the tomb of Tutankhamen was a model and a guide.

One of the pleasures of working in a large encyclopedic museum is the possibility to work across departments with experts in different fields, and I am grateful to my friend and colleague Kristen Gresh, Estrellita and Yousuf Karsh Curator of Photographs, for her advice in the selection of photographs.

Among my colleagues in the photo studio and visual archives department who gave the project their wholehearted support, I am grateful to Debra LaKind, Greg Heins, Jennifer Riley, John Woolf, David (Stoney) Stone, and Lisa Terrat. My regular visits to the photo studio to deliver materials for imaging were always a pleasure, and I would happily linger there looking over the scans and discussing our latest "finds" with John, Stoney, and Lisa.

Support for the scanning came from the Gertrude F. Shelley Fund for Ancient Egyptian Art and the Lotus Society, with additional funding from Helen Shaplin Dechtiar and J. Parker Prindle. Generous support for this publication was provided by the Egyptian Publication Fund at the Museum of Fine Arts, Boston.

Lawrence M. Berman
Norma Jean Calderwood Senior Curator of Ancient Egyptian, Nubian, and Near Eastern Art
Museum of Fine Arts, Boston

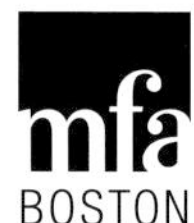

BOSTON

MFA Publications
Museum of Fine Arts, Boston
465 Huntington Avenue
Boston, Massachusetts 02115
www.mfa.org/publications

Generous support for this publication was provided by the Egyptian Publication Fund at the Museum of Fine Arts, Boston.

ISBN 978-0-87846-854-6
Library of Congress Control Number: 2018934531

The Museum of Fine Arts, Boston, is a nonprofit institution devoted to the promotion and appreciation of the creative arts. The Museum endeavors to respect the copyrights of all authors and creators in a manner consistent with its nonprofit educational mission. If you feel any material has been included in this publication improperly, please contact the Department of Rights and Licensing at 617 267 9300, or by mail at the above address.

While the objects in this publication necessarily represent only a small portion of the MFA's holdings, the Museum is proud to be a leader within the American museum community in sharing the objects in its collection via its website. Currently, information about approximately 400,000 objects is available to the public worldwide. To learn more about the MFA's collections, including provenance, publication, and exhibition history, kindly visit www.mfa.org/collections.

For a complete listing of MFA publications, please contact the publisher at the above address, or call 617 369 3438.

All illustrations in this book were produced by the Imaging Studios, Museum of Fine Arts, Boston, except where otherwise noted.

Edited by Jennifer Snodgrass
Proofread by Kathryn Blatt
Designed by Daphne Geismar
Production by Terry McAweeney
Production assistance by Anne Levine
Printed on 150 gsm Garda Premium Natural
Printed and bound at Graphicom, Verona, Italy

Distributed in the United States of America and Canada by
ARTBOOK | D.A.P.
75 Broad Street, Suite 360
New York, New York 10004
www.artbook.com

Distributed outside the United States of America and Canada by
Thames & Hudson, Ltd.
181A High Holborn
London WC1V 7QX
www.thamesandhudson.com

First edition
Printed and bound in Italy
This book was printed on acid-free paper.

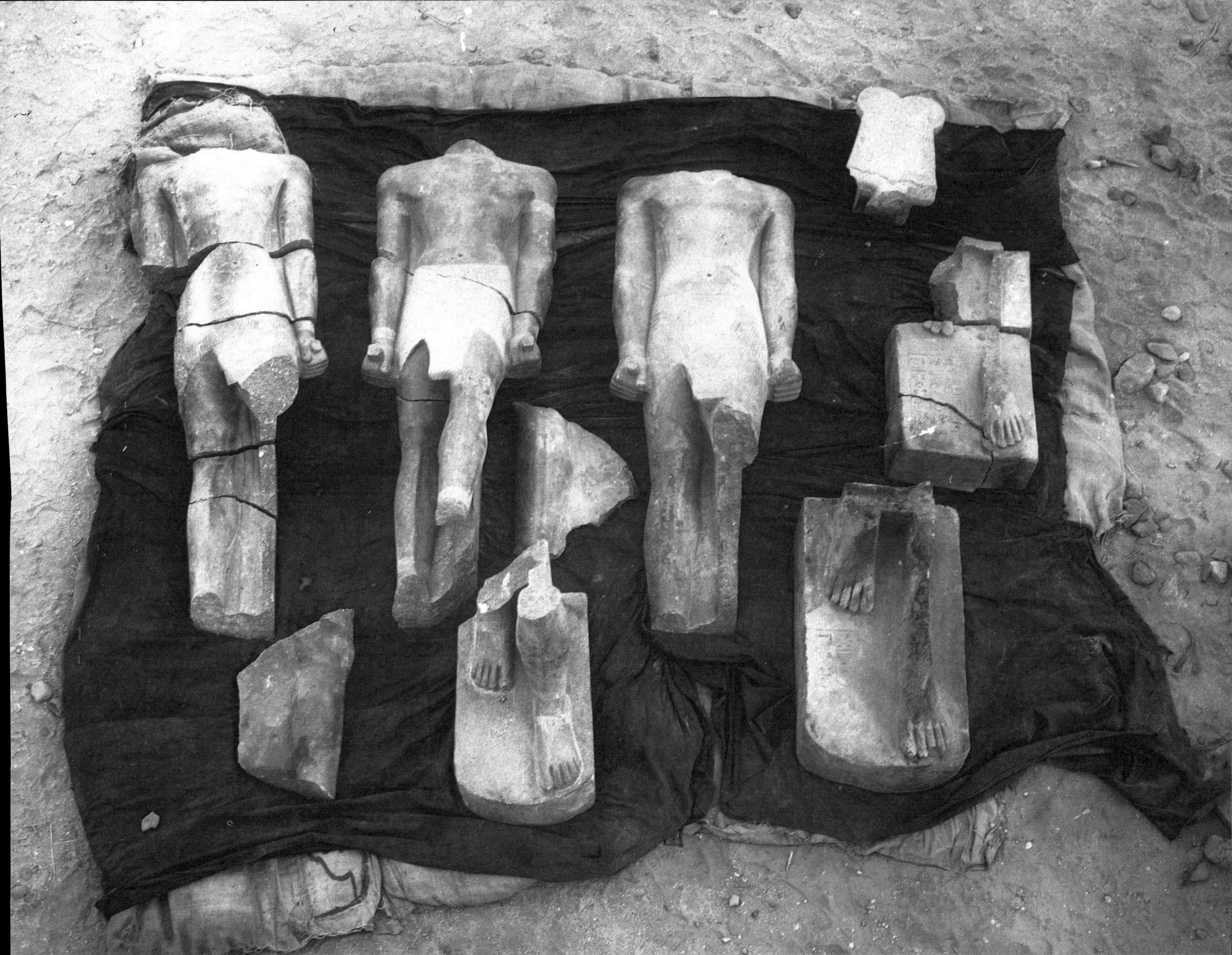